As a black corporate executive he helped expand the marketing focus of a Fortune 500 company

His leadership helped to alter the face of higher education in Union County, New Jersey

His presidency of two national organizations led to historic contributions

His achievements in public education earned state and national attention

A true leader in bringing promise and hope to educationally and economically disadvantaged seeking higher education

Others Thought I Could Lead

OTHERS THOUGHT I COULD LEAD

An Autobiography by **James S. Avery, Sr.**

A success story in corporate, educational, fraternal, and social/civic life

Others Thought I Could Lead

Published by Wheatmark®
610 East Delano Street, Suite 104
Tucson, Arizona 85705 U.S.A.
www.wheatmark.com

International Standard Book Number: 1-58736-578-2
Library of Congress Control Number: 2005937630

This book is dedicated to my beautiful wife, Joan Avery, who for 29 years of marriage, in her most loving and unselfish way, has been by my side, the living spirit who has given real definition to my life. Throughout it all, she has provided that special kind of insight, literary color, and guidance that all such endeavors require.

Contents

Preface. xi

Foreword xiii

My Heritage. 1

Life in My Hometown 13

Childhood Years 25

High School Years 39

Hail Columbia 49

Military Service 55

Back to Columbia 81

Playing Sports, Teaching, Coaching. 87

Entering the Business World 105

Becoming an Omega Man 109

Participating in Plainfield's Civic Life 113

Education and Race 117

The National Association of Market Developers,
Inc. (NAMD) 133

Doing More "Educating" at Humble Oil. 141

Working with the United Negro College Fund 145

Plans for Progress 153

Speaking Out 159

The Union County New Jersey Project 165

Moving Up in Omega's Leadership 175

More Educating and More Education .203

Guiding Exxon's Public Affairs in the 1970s 207

More Challenges 211

Speeches and Honors 223

Appointments in Higher Education. 233

Getting Personal Again. 237

An Important Addendum 247

Other Photographs of Interest in the Life of James S. Avery 249

Preface

This is a life story chronicled by a person who tried hard to make a real difference in the world around him and who seized opportunities for service and community participation which came to him as huge challenges.

Hopefully the reader will see this life story as an achievement of merit, built with respect, dignity, and purpose. I want to thank all my fraternity brothers, and other friends and business associates, who have encouraged and supported me along the way.

I could not have put this autobiography together in such a readable fashion without the assistance of some wonderful people including my wife, Joan, whose ability on the computer helped to make this book possible. The photographic history recorded in this book is largely due to four fraternity brothers: Rudy W. Powell, the late Felmon D. Motley, George T. Smith, Sr., for the documentation of district and national events, and George Williams for his photographic mastery at the international level. I want to thank my beloved fraternity brother, Horace Baldwin, for his insight and his literary expertise, Lianne Berkhold, my wife's cousin, for her outstanding professional editorial skills, and brother Ron Moffitt and his lovely wife Angie for their professional assistance in seeing this project through to completion.

Foreword

by Horace Baldwin

Cranford, a small, quiet town set in the suburban area of central New Jersey, is the opening setting of a life story of humble beginnings that ultimately makes an indelible impact upon society, as we know it today. The life is that of James S. Avery, and though not as widely known as Martin Luther King, Jr., Jim also made a significant contribution to the eradication of racism in America. James Avery's contribution to corporate America is not as highly regarded as that of Leon Sullivan—founder of the prototypical black self-help program Opportunities Industrialization Centers of America (OIC). But, Leon Sullivan was one of his contemporaries, and what Avery did as a corporate marketing executive opened many doors for many blacks and profoundly changed the marketing strategy throughout the corporate world.

Jim was raised in Cranford and in the pages of this book are many parallels to small town life as commonly popularized in American folklore. Neighborhood children playing sports and other games, hardworking parents, and strong religious beliefs are just a few of the iconic references we Americans treasure. Yet, as common as these references are, they are made special through the life of an exceptional black child, who never let obstacles interfere with the pursuit of his dream. Though raised in New Jersey, Jim has Southern roots that can be traced back to slavery. As such, the story of his life, the challenges he faced, and his ultimate accomplishments are characterized by determination, not resentment. Benjamin E. Mays captured the essence of this philosophy when he said: *"People with dreams know no poverty. Each of us is as rich as our dreams."*

In the early decades of the twentieth century, America was still a country with strong ethnic diversity. Although the South was more evident of racial segregation, many northern communities also had strong divisions along ethnic lines. For example, Little Italy, Little Havana, and Chinatown are examples of names used to describe respective neighborhoods. Yet, the town that Jim Avery grew up in reflected a cross-section of ethnic diversity, bound by people of modest means, a strong sense of community, and big dreams. This early adaptation to ethnic diversity played an important part in molding him into the leader he was to become.

If you look closely into this "All-American Community" as illustrated in this book, a picture will be painted for you reflecting the good, the bad, perhaps even the ugly. If we are not a perfect people, it can be deduced that there is no such thing as a perfect neighborhood. This patchwork of human existence called diversity is what makes ours a great nation. The core of this existence is the family, and if we are lucky, family is the basis of principles, which will guide our lives.

Jim Avery has always been a modest man. Even the title of this book reflects the acceptance of a fact confirmed by others rather than a proclamation of personal accomplishment. This does not mean that he is shy or one who trembles when faced with a challenge. He is a man comfortable with himself, able to speak candidly of his character, and willing to let the work he's done and the lives he's touched speak for him. This book captures his life's work and demonstrates his far-reaching influence.

The reader of this book has the opportunity to look introspectively and ask the following questions: What links us as a people? What links us as a country? What principles are important to live by? What makes a great leader? The story of this life shines a light on each of these questions, giving every one of us the opportunity to make a difference in our own way. In addition, there's the realization that leaders are not always the one out front in the spotlight or the individual at the microphone. Sometimes, it takes a powerful leader to work behind the scenes, networking through appropriate channels. James Avery was able to do both with equal fervor.

It has been said: *"those who do not study history are damned to repeat it."* The story of James Avery is living history from which current and future generations can learn. For example, to make an impact on a national scale takes a grass roots approach at the local level. One such cause championed by Jim at the local level was sickle cell anemia. His efforts during the sixties and those of others like him helped to elevate this issue to a national concern. Though the problem still exists, greater awareness and preventive measures have significantly reduced the incidence of new cases. Also, in October 2004, some forty years after the grass roots approach, the Federal government issued a postage stamp further raising awareness to sickle cell disease.

The story of *Others Thought I Could Lead* is quite capable of being successful just based upon the information shared above. However, it is much more than can be adequately described in an introduction. There's the personal side of James Avery, a side not often shared with the public. There is also the global focus on environmental issues, to which his commitment was just as strong as to race relations.

The essence of James S. Avery is captured in the principles of the international fraternal organization he was privileged to lead. Used since 1911, the principles of Manhood, Scholarship, Perseverance, and Uplift each carry a significant meaning to the men of Omega Psi Phi Fraternity. Jim possessed each characteristic prior to his affiliation with the organization and has since leveraged his influence to be a positive, living role model of each trait to everyone he comes in contact with—regardless of gender, race, or economic condition.

James S. Avery, Sr.

As future generations reflect on the list of leaders that made America great, the name James S. Avery will be on the list. Any detailed assessment of the criteria of influence common to the struggle of blacks must consider his contributions. Sometimes subtle, often far-reaching, his contributions are permanently entwined in the fabric of American life.

I sincerely thank my dear friend and brother James S. Avery for writing this book and sharing his story with the world. It is a classic American story rich in history, personal struggles, successes, failures, and the triumph of personal commitment. More importantly, everyone that reads this book has the opportunity to put his or her own story in perspective. There is so much that still needs to be done and so much each of us is capable of giving. Now is the time for the rest of us to make our mark or at least start the process. Let the next chapter begin with you!

Horace Baldwin

I

My Heritage

"You drew your first ever breath of life," my mother often told me, "with the smack of Dr. Friend Gilpin's hand on the cheek of your backside." The day was March 24, 1923, and the place was one of the two small upstairs bedrooms at 47 Johnson Avenue, Cranford, New Jersey. It was a long way from the slave cabin in Prince George County, Virginia, where my grandfather, James P. Polk Avery, was born. He was born a slave in 1845 and incredibly was owned by his own father, Colonel John Avery, a white plantation owner in Prince George County. My grandmother was one of Colonel Avery's many slaves.

The house where I was born was the same one my father had built when he came up from Virginia in 1908. In his early adult years, my father had worked in Petersburg, Virginia, for a firm called Friend & Company, which sold building materials such as wood, sand, and stone, and he had learned a great deal about carpentry. He single-handedly built the house on Johnson Avenue, and it still stands, with some modifications, nine decades later. He built the house on an acre of land, in the middle of six large oak trees with trunks the size of washtubs. Their branches seem to hover high above the roof as if protecting it from dangers.

The house is wood framed and has a porch across the front. When I was a child, you entered the front door and to the right you stepped into a small living room with a player piano in it. From the front hall you turned left into a larger sitting room that later became a bedroom. A dining room, a kitchen, and a tiny room off the back of the hall, which ran from the front door to the rear, made up the remainder of the space that defined the first floor. There was an "L"-shaped narrow porch that could be reached by two doors Father had put in leading out of the kitchen to the rear of the house. Upstairs was a very small bathroom with a toilet, a tub, and washbasin, two bedrooms, and a small room that was more like a large open closet. There was a cot in that small room that was used as "guest quarters" whenever a relative came up to visit. The kitchen had a big dark iron stove that was fueled by coal or wood, and there was a real icebox that held a small block of ice each day to keep things from spoiling. To reach the attic, you had to be tall enough to grab the rope and pull down the steps. By the time I was 12, even I could not stand up in the attic without banging my head on one of the beams. There was a small window on each end of the attic but there were no shelves, just space for old clothes and what might be called "keepable junk"! The basement, where my mother did the laundry and hung the clothes, had an earthen floor which had rivulets of water running through it when it rained.

At the time of my birth, I became the seventh person to live in that small house my father built, and for the life of me, I don't know how we did it. I was the last of five children born to Martha Ann Jones Avery and John Henry Avery. First there was Alice, named after our father's mother, then John H., named after our father. Then came Friend Phillip, named after the white family doctor, Dr. Friend P. Gilpin, and then Louis Nathaniel, named after father's brother. I was named after the grandfather who had been born into slavery. Not only was I the last child but I might have been an afterthought since I was born when my mother was 36 years of age. That happened to be seven years after Louis came into the world and thirteen years after Alice was born. I was always considered the baby boy and was looked after by my older brothers and sister.

My mother and my father were both born in Virginia. Mother, whose maiden name was Martha Ann Jones, was born in a rural area known as Cumberland County on March 12, 1887. The Jones family lived in a part of the county not far off Route 60 that was defined by rotting shacks and small houses where doghouses and outhouses gave a special character to the backyards. My mother, the daughter of Beverly and Rosa Jones, was a tall, attractive, light-skinned woman whom

I adored and who greatly influenced my life. I did not know much about my mother's background or that of her family beyond her five brothers, Edward, Joggasin, Emmet, Kinny, and Willis, and two sisters, Dolly and Charlotte. The day my mother died in February of 1941, Charlotte, whom we called Lottie and thought was an aunt, claimed that Mother told her on her death bed that she was not my mother's sister but her own daughter. That was never cleared up as far as my siblings and I were concerned. Whenever we talked about it, it was always with a sense of wonder and an attitude of not rocking the boat. No one ever checked the birth records, if there were any at all. If Lottie was correct, then she would have been born before my mother moved to New Jersey and met my father. When I spoke about my mother's family with her sister, Aunt Dolly, several years before Aunt Dolly's death, she would not talk about Lottie's claim, as if it were some deep, dark secret. I did not like that because the silence gave people the opportunity to dream up answers that may have had no substance or veracity. My aunt, Dolly Fleming, had five children, Jean, Annie, John, Rache, and Joseph. As I grew up I saw Jean and John more often than the others, but all of them were wonderful people who raised successful children, most of whom were college graduates with productive lives in the fields of education and business.

All of the Joneses were hardworking rural people and most of them labored on the farms in the area. Joggasin took care of the 55-acre family farm that was out behind the outhouse. He had a sway back mule with which he tilled the soil. I remember his telling us about those occasions when that mule had a lot of gas. He always dreaded those times, walking with the plow behind that mule, and his stories made us laugh. Edward, Emmet, and Willis were also farm laborers. Only Kinney did not work on a farm but was a barber in a small local shop just off Route 60. None of the Joneses appeared to have gone beyond the early grades in elementary school or to be anything but dirt poor. You would never know it by their demeanor, however, as they were the happiest, kindest, and most fun-filled people who told the funniest "knee-slapping" stories and kept life around them filled with laughter.

Taken at the farm in Cumberland, Virginia showing me (left) and two of my brothers, Johnny and Friend (right) posing with Uncle Kinney and Uncle Joggasin

My father, John Henry Avery, was born on December 23, 1873, in Petersburg, Virginia, a thriving, commercial city located in southeast Virginia along the Appomattox River south of Richmond. My father had one sister named Rosa, a brother Louis, and two half-sisters, Elizabeth and Louise, and a half-brother named Martin. Rosa, Louis, and John were children of my grandfather's first wife, whose name was Alice. Elizabeth, Louise, and Martin were the offspring of the second wife, Patience. I was told that she had two other baby boys who died at birth. She named each boy she had Martin until the third one survived.

My grandfather, James K. Polk Avery, was born when James Knox Polk was president of the United States and must have been given the James K. Polk name by his father. Since my grandfather had been a slave, he was given the last name of his father, Colonel Avery. The Colonel, who was a Virginian, must have fought for the Confederacy. I was told that my grandfather lived on a plantation in Prince George County outside of Petersburg where his father, Colonel Avery, according to statistical records for 1860 in Virginia, owned over one hundred slaves. Historical records obtained from the Petersburg,

Virginia, public library indicate that a John Avery, the son of Edward Avery, Jr., grew up on a plantation in Martins Brandon Parish in Prince George County, Virginia. Edward, Jr., was named after his father, Edward Avery, Sr., who died June 9, 1790.

Apparently, my grandfather had privileges because the overseers were instructed never to beat him. At the time of the "Crater Explosion" in Petersburg, he had been asked to take a horse and wagon into town to get some supplies from a store on Bollingbrook Street. This occurred during the Civil War. Historical records indicate that on July 30, 1864, an explosion occurred in a large mine under part of the Confederate works in a section of Petersburg. Troops from the Union Forces of General Ambrose E. Burnside's brigade of volunteers poured into the Crater but were driven out with heavy losses. Fortunately, my grandfather escaped without harm. Petersburg underwent a partial siege that lasted until April 3, 1865, when a general assault on the Petersburg lines finally broke General Robert E. Lee's resistance. Lee's forces surrendered. I have no information to indicate whether Colonel Avery was involved in the battles in Petersburg. On that same day that Lee's resistance was broken in Petersburg, Union forces entered Richmond. Lee surrendered the remnants of his army at Appomattox Courthouse a week later.

My grandfather, James K. Polk Avery, with his second wife, Patience, and two of their three children, Martin and Elizabeth

My grandfather died on March 14, 1916. The photograph I have of him with his second wife, Patience, and the three children shows him as a handsome, well-dressed, rather dignified-looking man. The photograph appeared to have been taken by a photographer who posed him with his wife and two of their children. He worked in a tobacco factory after his marriage to Patience, but he must have been illiterate because a deed for a $500 dollar loan he and Patience obtained in 1895 shows she signed her name next to his "X."

Patience, born on Easter Sunday in 1863, was a very attractive lady who was raised in Massachusetts by a white family. While in New England she received an education and learned the social graces. I could not find out any more about her or how she met my grandfather and fell in love with him. Patience Martin Avery died on August 1, 1940, at the age of 77.

Maybe it was because of Colonel John Avery that my father's eyes were blue as were the eyes of my brother Friend, my sister Alice, and me. It was obvious to me that my father and his brothers and sisters all had the advantage of better living conditions in Petersburg. You could tell by their dress, their demeanor, and outlook on life that they appeared to be more cultured and better educated than those in my mother's family.

My father's brother Louis married a lady whose first name was Emma. I know nothing about her. They had no children. I never knew about Uncle Louis's occupation. Every time I saw him, he looked like a well-dressed dignified sort that would have held a job that required nice clothing, like being a maitre d' in a restaurant. My father's sister, Aunt Rosa, had been married too. Her name was Rosa Davenport. She was light skinned, fair haired, and an extremely gentle and kind person. Rosa had four children, Henry, Manuel, Lizzie, and Fanny, but I could not find out any more about them. I was in Aunt Rosa's small cottage on Bollingbrook Street in Petersburg several times when

Louis Avery, my uncle and my father's brother, in Petersburg, VA (circa 1935)

I was growing up but never met any of her children. Uncle Lee Martin Avery, Dad's half brother, whom we called Martin, was born August 11, 1892. He was a very likeable, warm natured person who never married or had any children. He died in August of 1985 when he was 93 years of age.

Aunt Elizabeth, my father's half sister, was born on March 30, 1895. She married a fellow named Russell Holmes. I liked Russell. He was a savvy guy, a skilled man who was a building contractor and put up some of the finest homes in the City of Petersburg. In fact, Russell Holmes was the first black contractor in the state of Virginia to receive an award for his construction work. Interestingly, their home was not a large, pretentious one like those he built for whites in the state, although it was meticulously neat and filled with lovely furniture. Whenever I went to Petersburg, I looked forward to staying with Aunt Elizabeth and Uncle Russell. They never had any children, but they did raise one of Aunt Louise's three boys, Ashton.

Aunt Louise, the youngest of the three, was born September 19, 1904. She first married a fellow whose last name was Morrison. She met him while she was a student at Hampton Institute. He was a tailor but as the years passed he was not a very responsible or supportive husband and father. He squandered his money and made life miserable for Aunt Louise. She later divorced him and married a man named Walter Dennis. I met Walter, but all I remember is that he was a well-spoken, intelligent man who worked for the state beverage control board. Aunt Louise had three sons. The oldest was Ashton, and the other two boys were named Avery and Holmes. Mr. Dennis was a good stepfather who saw to it that the boys attended Virginia State College. In the late 1990s when my wife Joan and I were living in Edison, New Jersey, we used to see my cousin Holmes Morrison when we walked in the park in South Plainfield. Holmes lived in Plainfield, New Jersey, and was a very good actor in the theater. I remember that he once told us he had just finished a role in Shakespeare's play *Othello* and in several productions played the chauffeur in *Driving Miss Daisy*. He has since moved to Raleigh, North Carolina, where he is still active in the theater. Ashton and Avery still live in Petersburg. Both of my aunts, Elizabeth and Louise, are deceased, but I cannot recall the dates of their deaths.

When I reflect upon my heritage, I am frankly distressed that I know so little about my family's past. In the days when I was growing up, I do not recall my family discussing details of their backgrounds, and I did not have the foresight to ask. While I have talked with cousins Avery, Holmes, and Ashton recently, I have not had the opportunity to see them in person in recent years, something that I deeply regret. I was 81 years of age in March of 2004 and knew that I had better make an effort to seek more information for my children and grandchildren while I can.

In October of 2004, I went to the funeral of my cousin Annie Fleming, who was one of Aunt Dolly's children. I had the opportunity to meet cousins from Vermont, Staten Island, Brooklyn, South Orange and East Orange, New Jersey, Maryland, and Virginia. All of them were descendants of Aunt Dolly's five children, all well educated, some with college degrees, including master's and doctorates. Isn't it ironic that it took a death, this time Annie's, to bring relations together in a way that made all of us feel the significance of family ties. I felt saddened that I had these wonderful relatives that I did not know and may not have the chance to strengthen the bonds that link us so interminably together.

It was not until my father was 35 years of age that he came to New Jersey in 1908. That same year he met and married my mother, who was then 21 years old. They first met at a wedding of a mutual friend and after a brief courtship married on April 7, 1908. My father was an extremely handsome, quiet, dignified man who was devoted to his family. Every person he came in contact with liked and respected him. He never had an enemy his whole life. He was a very hard worker who did yard work, some house painting, and general cleanup for homes on the other side of Cranford.

Both my mother and father were religious people. They were Baptists and attended the First Baptist Church in Cranford. Just like many other Christian families, my father enjoyed blessing the food before we began to eat. It was a practice that my brothers, Friend and Louis, kept doing until their death. My father never raised his voice in criticism or to reprimand any of us. It was as if he was blessed with a kind of quiet dignity that in its relative silence garnered huge respect from all of the family. My mother was the vocal boss of the household and the one who directed us religiously and otherwise. When I was old enough to speak, my mother taught me the prayer, " Now I lay me down to sleep, I pray the Lord my soul to keep. If I die before I wake, I pray the Lord my soul to take." For many years, I said that prayer every night at the side of my bed before going to sleep. Mother often talked to me about God and His goodness and how He always blessed those who loved Him. She made sure that I went to Sunday school every Sunday. When I was eleven years old I was baptized in the small pool under the altar of the First Baptist Church on High Street in Cranford, New Jersey.

My sister Alice, the first born, could read music and loved to play the piano. I don't remember how she learned to play. I believe she had some lessons in her early youth. Many a Sunday afternoon and some other times, too, you could hear Alice on the piano with my mother and Lottie singing hymns like, "His Eye Is on the Sparrow" and another with the words, "Precious Lord Take My Hand, Lead Me On." Those were two hymns that my mother loved and were sung often. Religion was important in the Avery household but not to the point of being a Bible-thumping, shouting regularity. In fact, there never was any shouting as one would hear in a revival meeting, nor any reading aloud of the Bible. The Bible was just accepted as an authority for living and was the basis of what was heard or read in church or at home about God and the rules of life.

Father remained a Baptist until the middle 1930s when he apparently disagreed with some of the church policies of Reverend Benjamin J. Allen, the minister. In what was perhaps the most demonstrative thing he ever did, "Dear," as many in the family called Dad, changed over to the African Methodist Episcopal Church on High Street in Cranford and became a Methodist. He attended faithfully until his death in the summer of 1959. Mother, for reasons I never knew, stopped going to church on Sundays, but she remained a deeply religious person. It was rumored that she had what old folks called a "falling out" with some of the church deaconesses.

I could understand my father having a problem with Reverend Allen. The Reverend was a very stubborn and somewhat condescending man. I remember that after World War II we had a softball team in the town that played in the local summer league. We were quite good and received a lot of publicity. The team was made up of fellows who went to either the Baptist or Methodist church and others who went to neither. I was the captain of the team, and the Reverend called me one day and said he wanted to buy the team jerseys with First Baptist Church on the back. I told him we couldn't do that for some of the guys went to the Methodist Church and others didn't attend anywhere. He said he would destroy the team by making sure that many of the boys who attended First Baptist would no longer play. Imagine a minister saying such a thing! His threat did not work. I never felt the same about Reverend Allen after that episode. I always wondered how he could separate the Christian things he said on Sunday from the non-Christian things he said during the week. Christian living to me was an everyday thing and was something I learned from my mother, not Reverend Allen.

In spite of that, I have to say Reverend Benjamin J. Allen, although he had some odd ways about him, was a true innovator. He was ahead of his time for the kind of ministry he advocated. He felt the church was the means to effect real economic change among blacks in the community. Central to his ideas was the formation of the first credit union in any black church in New Jersey and perhaps the nation. He felt the credit union was not only a way to save, he felt it was a way to borrow and to use funds on behalf of the community and its members. It was his idea to buy coal in large bulk supplies more cheaply than individuals could obtain it and make the coal available at a lower cost to church members. The credit union is still in operation and continues doing very well today, some 70 years after its formation. I still participate as a member of the Credit Union's Audit Committee. The whole idea of economic empowerment today for the black community was something that Reverend Allen had in mind almost three-quarters of a century ago.

I never realized in my elementary school years that the religious upbringing my parents gave me, making me attend Sunday School and church services and having me baptized and emphasizing the importance of Christian living in the home, all gave me a Christian foundation that has never left me. While I was brought up in the Baptist denomination, I have always seen my relationship with God as an individual one in the sense that I can feel religiously comfortable praying alone and consulting Him on a one-to-one basis. I cannot say that I am an "A" student when it comes to practicing all the right things that makes one a good Christian model, though I wish I could. There are times when my compassion is not what it should be, and there are times when the need to give of myself is lacking in depth and dimension. In fact, I can be downright selfish at times, unwilling to share unless it is something that benefits me. I do not consider that to be a serious fracture in character, but it is something of which I am not proud.

II

Life in My Hometown

Cranford, New Jersey, the town I lived in until adulthood, was created by the New Jersey Legislature as a township in March 1871. By the time I came along, it was a small town of ten thousand people with the Rahway River ambling and twisting its way slowly through it. The river played an important recreational role as the town developed. People enjoyed using the Rahway River for canoeing especially in the early evening. On special occasions there were canoe-tilting contests, canoe regattas, and colorful river carnivals. People came from all over to see the canoes and river crafts decorated with colorful materials and Japanese lanterns as they paraded in the river from Eastman Street to the dam near Casino Avenue. Cranford, often called the Venice of New Jersey, is located in Union County, New Jersey. It is nestled between Garwood, Roselle, Linden, and Kenilworth and right along the New Jersey Central Railroad that ran from Bound Brook to Jersey City, New Jersey, where people could take the ferry to New York City. Trolley tracks that began in Dunellen, New Jersey, ran through the town down South Avenue and curled up over some B&O freight tracks before continuing on through Roselle. Where the trolley crossed over the B&O tracks, there was a baseball field that held a lot of sports history dealing with blacks. It was enclosed with wooden fencing and had bleachers on both sides. During the late spring and summer, every Sunday when the weather was good, one of the traveling black baseball teams would come to play an exhibition game with a local team of black players called the Dixie Giants. I remember seeing the Birmingham Black Barons, the Indianapolis Clowns, the St. Louis Monarchs, and teams from Philadelphia and Richmond who came to play there. It was great fun. People came from all over the county, particularly "colored folks" (as they called us then), came with picnic baskets with food of all sorts and blankets, too, in case all the seats were taken, for a wonderful afternoon of baseball. The team managers always passed the hat to collect what they could to help pay expenses of the visiting teams. We saw some fine black players of major league quality, but we never realized we were looking at some true Americana history. If you look at that area today, there is no trolley overpass or playing field. An industrial building fills most of the space with some smaller businesses in adjoining areas. That chapter of Americana and baseball history is gone and apparently forgotten.

Cranford did not have any industry until after World War II, and at that, it was small industry. It was essentially a bedroom community for people who worked in New York City, in various New Jersey cities, and in the factories in neighboring towns like Garwood, Kenilsworth, and Linden. A number of the men who lived on Johnson Avenue, where I lived, worked at Thatchers Iron Works on South Avenue in Garwood, a place where the ore was melted and shaped into forms that ended up as furnaces. Many evenings the top of the main building would open up and you could see industrial smoke and particles of fire from the splashing of molten steel rising like sparklers on the Fourth of July into the clear, evening sky. While this scene was a delight to those of us watching it in those days, environmental standards have since become far more stringent and today that company would be severely fined for its emissions.

The railroad, which was called the Central Railroad of New Jersey, had a centrally located station in the town and Cranford was a local stop. I can recall the steam locomotives that belched up dense black smoke as they chugged out of the station. I remember the loud, piercing train whistles of the express trains that raced through the town. I was really fascinated with the trains when they were later modernized and ran by diesel instead of coal. The Meteor, the classiest model with its shiny bullet-like engine, was really something to see on a beautiful, cold moonlit evening as it raced through town with its special horn noisily expressing its pride at being the best of the line!

The Central Jersey RR divided the town. People on the north side of the tracks were mostly the upper middle class and the rich who lived in large, imposing houses on many of the tree-lined streets like Casino Avenue and Prospect Street. The great majority of those on the south side, where we lived, were the working class poor. Naturally, the south side had almost all of the blacks who lived in the town. A goodly share lived right on Johnson Avenue, but, interestingly enough, Johnson Avenue was not a segregated street. The Limones, an Italian family, lived in a home next to ours on one side and a Polish family lived next to us on the other side. The Nemeths, a Hungarian family, lived next to them and further up the street lived the Addoutties, more Hungarians, and the Iannocones, another Italian family. The Keetches lived three houses from ours down the street. I don't remember whether they were Scottish or German. I know they were not black. The Keetches, who did not have any children, were extremely well liked by everybody. I could not tell you why, but the house where the Keetches lived seemed to be the line at which interracial living ended. From that point on, the residents were totally black. One could clearly associate the depth of one's poverty along racial lines, yet, it was an environment that had no incidents of racial bias. Everyone just seemed to get along, minding their own business. Those of us who lived "up the street," were often in each other's homes and shared each other's happy times and sad ones too. I am sure some bias existed covertly but there still was enough contact and interaction to move one's perception closer to reality and to help one's understanding more about a person individually. This was ironic at a time in America when prejudice, discrimination, and even things like lynchings were still part of the moral landscape.

One of the things I remember most about that neighborhood and those times was the fact that, despite the economic conditions of some people and the differences that may have existed in family life, families still remained intact, interdependent, and loyal. Sure, some youngsters got into trouble, nothing very serious, but they were disciplined in the home and the punishment for the wrongdoing was often quite painful. Fathers remained in the home, responsible for income generation.

Mothers, of course, were the supreme authority in the family. The Hurtt, the Carter, and the Mayer families, all with five to seven children, were excellent examples of this. How different from today wherein so many black men have fathered children and not remained in the home to help raise them. Far too often black men have given in to circumstances of failure and have lost their dignity as true fathers and as real men.

I believe living in this multicultural environment gave me a state of readiness to deal with people not on any superficial basis of race or color, but rather on their character traits as human beings. As I grew up into adulthood, I was never uncomfortable among any group, and I judged a person for what he or she displayed as an individual. Conversely, as I grew into adulthood, I saw the impact of abject conditions of poverty and the lack of education spawn a sense of hopelessness and anger in many blacks who lived in the urban areas. It bred a feeling of inferiority that was like an indelible stain that forever marked their thinking and their own self-image. The more I saw this happening, the more I wanted immunity from ever being infected with this condition. In fact, it was a constant motivational factor in my psyche that has always helped to guide my way.

There was a rather stark difference in the housing on Johnson Avenue. When you came around Elise Street onto Johnson Avenue, you could see on one side what we called the "flats," a long line of connected narrow row houses. As you progressed up the street, the housing became better and the grounds appeared greener and better kept. In a funny way, the people who lived up the street seemed to project a quality of existence that set them a cut above most of those who lived in the flats. This isn't to say that those in the flats were in any way ostracized for where they lived, just that their conditions of life appeared to be a lot more economically challenging.

Saturday nights on Johnson Avenue seemed to bring out the worst in some of those who lived down the street. It was not anything racial that caused the problems, it was that some of the men would drink too much liquor, start arguing about something, and end up fighting in the dust and dirt that made up the yard where grass should have grown in front of the flats. The police seemed to come every Saturday night to take someone away and jail them for the weekend for one reason or another.

The numbers, as they called a form of gambling, was a game of chance, similar to Lotto that is played today. Lotto like many other games of chance is now legal and is conducted by state authorities. Back when I was young, people would bet money on the hope that their "number" would be drawn. I don't think anybody ever knew who did the drawing or where their money ended up. Many who lived in the poorer sections of town played the numbers. Every once in a while the cops would arrest a numbers runner, take him down to the station house, and put him in jail for a few days for being involved in the numbers racket. They were never there long, and when they got out of jail they went right back to what they were doing before they were picked up. People welcomed them back happily so they could continue to seek their fortunes, hoping that their number would be the lucky one. Such gambling was not peculiar to people who lived on Johnson Avenue, for games of chance exist in all parts of the world. Gambling is a perpetual dream of people everywhere.

The lower end of Johnson Avenue always seemed to get the worst of it, even when we had torrential rains. A heavy rain would flood the street up to where the better housing began, but for some strange reason never went much further, making the lower end of Johnson Avenue impassable. We could never get out easily when such a rain came. My father, like other men on the street, had hip boots so he could wade through the water until it subsided. When the water went down, the lower end of the street would smell dank and moldy for a long time. The dankness never seemed to leave some of those cellars.

In growing up on Johnson Avenue, except for one strange thing, I never felt the differences in people that I noticed more readily in our country once I became an adult and went elsewhere. That exception was in the Cranford movie theater where for some unstated reason all the blacks sat in the upper left side of the movie house. It was the "colored folks'" own peculiar peanut gallery. There were isolated times when a black person would venture to sit somewhere else in the theater, but that practice appeared to be frowned upon by many blacks at the time. I often wondered what started the practice. Even Tommy and I sat in that designated area when we went to the movies as kids. Later, as a high school athlete, I sat with the team, not in the peanut gallery. I really believed that blacks sitting in that special area was an inherited behavior, a distinctive segregated pattern related to the comfort level of living separately that created an assumed feeling of inferiority or difference that made blacks feel more secure in a separate setting. That kind of behavior dissolved as racial equality increased in the United States.

Interestingly, Johnson Avenue today is still integrated, but even more so. Whites and blacks live down the street as well as up the street, reflecting the positive changes we see in so many of our towns and cities.

When I think back on those days, there were many things that were very different. Take, for example, the matter of life and death in the black community. Pregnancies and most illnesses ended in the home. Very few sick or pregnant people asked to go to a hospital where the cost was prohibitive for many of the poorer class. Women had their babies at home and a few selected women in the area (my mother was one of them) would help one of only two black doctors that serviced the community. One was Dr. Polk, who lived in Roselle, and the other was Dr. Brock, who lived in Westfield. I can still see Dr. Brock in his car with that big police dog he always had riding in the back seat. It may have been that Dr. Brock was carrying valuable medicine and used the dog for protection, but I really think he didn't want to leave that dog at home when he made house calls. Dr. Friend P. Gilpin (the one my brother Friend was named after) and another white doctor, Dr. Lewis, who had an office on Lincoln Avenue, made house calls too. Dr. Lewis was highly regarded. He attended to more black families on our street than any other doctor, white or black. In those days, most blacks did not go to the doctor's office, so the doctor would come to the house, particularly when someone was very sick or when a child was born. Many people who got very sick from various ailments died at home too. Going to a hospital was too expensive, and they didn't have the hospitalization that most people have today. For the most part, when they died, blacks did not have wakes in the funeral parlors nor were the parlors used for funeral services. The body was laid out in the living room of the home for friends and family to see and mourn over. You could always tell the house when it had a body in it because there was a large funeral wreath on the front door. The funerals themselves were held in the church where the person was a member. Often after the service the funeral procession would go slowly by the person's home before going on to the cemetery, as if giving that person one last chance to see their home.

I did not know much about burial costs at the time, but I do know that many adults on the block had burial insurance that cost only pennies a month. This barely provided for the grave in places like Fairview Cemetery in Westfield, New Jersey, much less for some kind of small stone. My mother had that kind of pennies-a-day insurance. A fellow from Progressive Life would come each week to get the 25 cents and record it in his book.

When I visit the graves of my mother and father, I see the names of many of those who lived on and around our street in Cranford. I don't know if the burial plots were in a special segregated area or if the poorer people were just put in the less favorable, cheaper land areas. Whatever the reason, they were all buried in the same general area. You could stand at one vantage point and see the graves of black people who lived in Cranford, people with names like Giles, Jones, Cox, Tucker, Taylor, Smock, and Townsend to name a few. The only whites I knew of that lived on Johnson Avenue and died while I was living there were Italian, and they were buried in Catholic cemeteries.

When I was growing up my mother worked as a domestic. She was a maid who worked in the homes of two families in town. My father was what you might call a generalist. He cut lawns, cleaned up places, beat rugs, painted homes and, if necessary, stoked furnaces and shoveled snow in the winter. Naturally, he did these things for people on the north or richer side of town. When he would beat rugs (people for the most part in those days had rugs not carpeted floors), he would do it out in the person's backyard on his knees with strong pliable switches. He would never just beat rugs "bam, bam, bam." He beat the rugs, doing a rhythmic rat-a-tat-battatty-bat drum solo. People going by on the sidewalk would stop and listen to him. I can still see him on his knees deeply engulfed in his work with the dust flying in all directions around him making like he was a Gene Krupa, the world famous jazz drummer.

My mother worked on both sides of town. On the north side of town she worked for a Mr. Denman, who commuted to his job in New York City. I will never forget Mr. Denman. The only real shoes I ever wore for many years were hand-me-downs that belonged to Mr. Denman. I always knew that I could never ask my mother to buy me my own pair of new shoes since my family never had extra money for such luxuries. On the south side of town, mother worked for the Babbitt family on Hillcrest Avenue. They were very nice people who had a great love and respect for my mother.

Although my parents didn't have very much money, somehow they made things do for the five of us. My father had a garden in our back yard and raised many of the vegetables we ate such as corn, potatoes, string beans, cabbage, and beets. Quite often mother would buy chickens from a man who sold them fresh off his truck. Not unlike many of our neighbors on the street, my father raised chickens in the back yard. Father would buy little newborn chicks from Schlecters Hardware Store downtown on South Avenue and keep them in the cellar until they had grown large enough to join the older chickens in the chicken coop we had in the rear of the yard. I remember going down to the hardware store to get the mash we fed the little biddies. The mash had a fragrance that mixed with the smell of newly sawed wood and plant seeds that melded into an ambrosia-like smell that pervaded the whole store. I loved helping to raise the young chicks and seeing them grow into roosters and hens. We kept all the egg-laying hens, but the other chickens were dinner entrées. It was on Sundays that we would have one of the unlucky chickens from the coop as the featured entrée at dinner. Early Sunday morning Father would bring the chicken in from the coop, take it down to the coal bin, lay the head on a wooden chopping block, and chop it off. I can still see that chicken flopping around the coal bin, blood draining from his throat, until he could flop no more. Mother would then take him, clean out the innards and put the chicken in very hot water until she could pluck out each feather and quill. That chicken's skin was so clean it looked like a fresh one you buy in a store. I always hated the smell of a chicken when plucking out all of the wet feathers, and I never offered to do that job, nor did I ever, ever chop the head off a chicken!

Two of my brothers, Johnny and Louis, present Mother's Day flowers to Mom in the yard at 47 Johnson Avenue, Cranford, NJ.

My mother was an amazing woman! She made all the soap we used, all the soda we drank, and all the bread, biscuits, cakes, pies, and rolls we ate. Once in a while, in the summer she made ice cream that was so, so good! She was a fabulous cook! Since we were quite poor, during the week we often ate things like baked beans, kidney beans, and beef stew dishes that could serve many people. There were times we had a meal of pork & beans, sliced bread, and milk, which was very filling and very economical. Everything mother made was delicious, but her fried chicken was beyond delicious. I could never find the words to express the wonderful taste of whatever she made. Of course, on Johnson Avenue, at least up where we lived, my mother's cooking was not the exception when it came to being good, it was the rule. Most of the mothers on that street could really cook. Mrs. Rhea Stevenson, my buddy Tommy Stevenson's mom, could also cook up a storm. Her cakes and pies were out of this world. I ate at Steve's house a lot. Many times at breakfast his mom would make toast with some aged cheddar cheese on it that was delicious. I could never duplicate it. She was like a second mother to me, especially after my own mother died on February 4, 1941.

When I reflect on those days, I marvel at the ingenuity displayed by most of the parents. I certainly saw that with my mom and dad. Most of the new clothing we wore was purchased out of a station wagon owned by Mr. Hobbie, a traveling clothing salesperson. He would come around each month, and mother would buy sparingly the clothing we needed. She would buy some chickens for stewing from one peddler and fresh caught porgies and white fish from another. Once in a while she would buy lobsters, something that my brothers loved, but I never ate. Pigs' feet and hog maws were cooked periodically. Again, they were parts of the pig I did not like and never ate. Another peddler in a vegetable truck sold the few other vegetables that my father didn't grow. Dugan's Bakery came around with the butter and milk we needed. Those were the days in the winter when the milk came in bottles with the cream on top and the cream would become semi solid and expand and push the cap up. I don't think my parents went down town to buy anything. Mother and Father bought these things each week from those peddlers with the dirt-poor wages they made being a maid and a handyman.

Each day on his way home from his work on the north side of town "Dear," my father, would stop at the local bakery and get the day old buns that the baker was planning to discard the next day. My father never had a car. He walked all over town pushing a wheelbarrow with his tools in it. He did this for all the years I can remember. Later in life, he did get a used bike that saved him some time in his travels. He never complained about not having the things other people had. He took life as it came to him and made the best of meager circumstances. Everybody knew Mr. Avery in town. He tipped his hat to all the ladies and spoke in friendly tones to men. My father was always a gentleman, displaying courtesy to everybody he met. He was a hard working man and during the week he looked it. His clothing during the week was always worn and somewhat tattered. Frankly, when I was young, I use to be a little ashamed of how disheveled he looked pushing his wheel barrel around town. As I grew into adulthood, admiration, love, and respect overwhelmed that stupid feeling I had when I was too young to know what was really important in judging another person, especially my dad. I often looked at my father when he was in his early eighties and wondered, how in hell could he have done it. Raking, mowing, digging, pushing a wheel barrel loaded with a manual lawnmower and heavy tools all across town. Some winter nights after a long day of working he would get up after a few hours sleep and go shovel out the driveways and sidewalks of the people he worked for before dawn arose. I never heard him moan about any aches and tired pains he must at times have felt. In my eyes when I looked at him then, he stood ten feet tall!

During the summers in the years before I went to high school, I helped him cut some of the lawns that he was responsible for. There were times when those lawns looked like a million acres of grass but somehow I got through the mowing and appreciated the money he gave me for helping him. I often think about my father and of those days of cutting grass and how I always seemed to feel far greater fatigue than he. Mostly, though, I think of his gentle, easy going nature and how wonderful a man he was throughout the years. I remember sleeping in the same bed with him as a youngster, and I remember the smell of the previous day's working sweat in the long johns that he always wore. The smell was never offensive to me. It was just symbolic of a man's responsibility as a man.

III

Childhood Years

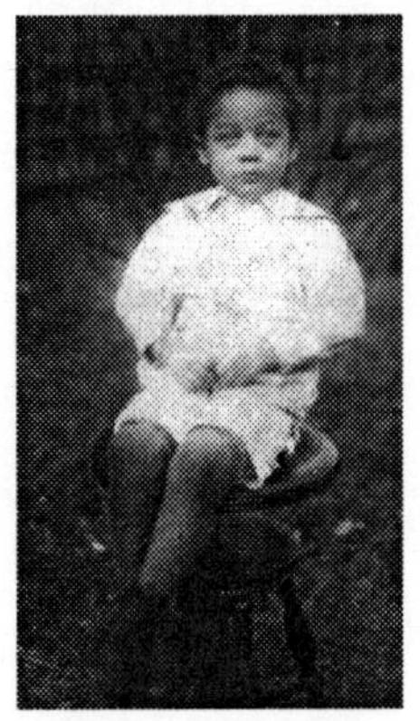

Sitting on a stool when I was three years old

For some five years after my birth, 47 Johnson Avenue was my entire universe. It was a nice, warm comfortable place. From the earliest times I can remember I felt a lot of love and nurturing, especially from my mother. Some might say she spoiled me because she made me feel special and wanted the best for me. My brothers and my sister and the one I called Aunt Lottie were like that too. While my mother doted on me, she was at the same time a strong disciplinarian. I was never allowed out of our yard when I began to walk and talk. When I did venture past that boundary, mother would use a switch on my legs to remind me of where I belonged. The switch was horrible and stung like bee bites, and I would cry as if I were dying. It was indeed rare that I made the stupid mistake to leave the property line; my fear of the switches was just too great.

In my early elementary years my yard was my playground. My friend Tommy Stevenson, who lived across the street, and I played ball in the front yard where we made first, second, and home bases because there wasn't enough room for third base. Most of the time I played alone in the rear of the house. Out by the vegetable garden I built a miniature baseball field with walls and a backstop. I fashioned 18 sticks into bats for each of the 18 ball players and used a steel ball, taken from a marble-shooting set, for the baseball. I made up big league teams and threw the ball with my right hand and swung the bat with my left. I set up leagues, played nine inning games, kept the scores as well as batting averages for each league, and maintained a schedule of games. All ground balls were outs. Pop ups were fly ball outs. Occasionally, the steel ball would sail over the outfield wall for a homer.

In the fall, I stuffed an old football that had no bladder inside with heavy rags, tied the leather strings and spent hours just kicking the ball back and forth in the side yard. That helped me learn how to kick a football so that it would sail high and spiral as it went. In the winter, I put a small basket with the bottom removed up against the outer post of the back porch and used a tennis ball to play basketball for hours. I improvised a lot. I did everything in the yard when I was young and in the early elementary grades. I even had a store on the back porch where I employed an old scale and made bins for the corn, small carrots, and beet stalks that would have been thrown away along with the unused kale. To me it was a grocery store where I could parcel out amounts, use an old scale to weigh them, give them a price per quarter, half and full pound and then sell them to make-believe customers. I had a great imagination and that same imagination led me to believe my parents when they told me about Santa Claus. I could hardly sleep on Christmas Eve since I was anxious to see what toy Santa would bring me. How difficult it must have been for my parents to see that each one of their five children had a gift on Christmas day.

It never bothered me that we were a poor family, never on welfare, but just poor. When I was a child, I saw other kids on the block in the same situation who had a number of rather large toys and bikes. I never had toys like that and never complained about it. Most of the things I had were used. Anything I had gotten new for everyday use I wore until they did not fit anymore or until the sneakers or clothes were worn through. I wore sneakers until there were holes in the soles and I had to put folded-over pages of old newspapers in the bottom to cover the holes. I wore them until the soles flapped up and down as I walked and made the sneakers not wearable. There were several times when a rusty nail left on the ground would pierce the bottom of my foot through the hole and through the paper. My mother would put a poultice on my foot to help prevent infection. Talk about a sore foot!

I am sure that some people who read this autobiography will wonder why the level of poverty did not impact my sense of being more deeply. Frankly, I just did not feel any strong sense of poverty, neglect, or deep need. Our home was clean, without rats or roaches. We were clean and adequately clothed. We never went without food. The love we felt was a warm and comforting kind of secure love that just made us feel whole and good. We never lost the pride and feeling of dignity in who we were. I don't know how to explain it any other way.

I started school in 1928 when I was five years old. It was a year before the Great Depression. Dressed up in a new shirt, pants, and my brother's shoes, early one September morning I went off proudly to kindergarten in Sherman School, a K to Eighth Grade school located on Lincoln Avenue. I still remember Mrs. Klace, my kindergarten teacher. She was perfect for kids who were beginning school, warm, friendly, and just plain nice and cuddly. I looked forward to going to school each day and doing the things she planned for us to do with crayons, paints, and beginning books.

Kindergarten was in the annex building where they also had special classes for kids that the teachers felt could not do well in regular classes. Most of the kids in those particular classes were black, some were from dysfunctional family situations with one parent or parents that had little education and less concern about formal education for their children. Some of them I am sure had the potential but didn't have anyone to encourage them and help them get the basics they needed to get by educationally. Some of the mothers had two, three, or more children. Some had to get welfare assistance. They appeared to be bathed in poverty and living in conditions that did not encourage any interest in learning to read or write well or to concentrate on learning at school. Once the boys reached the teenage years, a number of them quit going to school. One wonders how they could survive, make a good living, and avoid ending up in the human scrap heap of failure without basic education. When they later became adults and had children or got married and had children, they simply kept alive the stream of poverty and the lack of educational motivation or skill in their offspring.

What many people never talked about was the dreadful impact of covert prejudice that infected attitudes and the ability to get jobs, decent housing, and a good education. These things severely hurt one's ambition and outlook in some cases, killing any idea that things could actually get better. This sort of prejudice goes on today and unfortunately helps to keep many blacks and other poor people socially and economically handicapped. Many blacks succumbed to their own failures and were their own worst enemies when it came to trying to do better. They just seemed to give up trying, overwhelmed by the negativism that seemed to devour their will.

I saw a paper published in 2003 by the National Center for Educational Statistics, U.S. Department of Education, entitled: "Students Whose Parents Did Not Go To College." Just like the youngsters in those special classes years ago, with few exceptions, there is a continuing correlation today with children of parents who do not have college degrees. In 1999, according to the study, while 82% of students with parents with degrees enrolled in college, only 54% of students with parents without degrees enrolled in college. The percentages were much less for students of parents who did not finish high school.

Speaking of not finishing high school, none of my siblings completed the 12th grade. I know that my mother and father continually encouraged each of us to get an education. I know from what my sister and brothers have done in life that they were intelligent, perceptive people. Frankly, I have always believed that the reasons they did not finish high school were largely the fault of the attitude of most of their teachers. Many in society at that time, including those in education, just did not think black people could be anything more than blue-collar laborers.

My sister Alice and brothers Johnny, Friend, and Louis had good personalities and got along with everyone. In fact, I cannot ever remember any person with whom they ever had any trouble or difficulty. My sister had piano lessons and learned to play by reading the musical notes. Her penmanship and spelling were excellent. She did crossword puzzles all the time. When she was an adult, Alice was a seamstress and at one time was a partner in a small shop on North Avenue in Cranford. She did business with women all over town and had a great reputation. Louis loved to play with crystal sets getting radio station programs from far and wide. He would spend hours down in the basement working on old radios and other electrical devices. Later in life, Louis could fix any electrical problem, fix radios and TVs, and do most anything like that for various people. Louis worked as a buyer in the purchasing department of the Fidelity Union Bank and held the record there when he retired for having worked for 28 years without one sick day! Johnny could have gone much further with his education too. As a young man, Johnny worked in a variety store in down town Cranford. He saved his money and bought himself a Model T with a rumble seat. It was a symbol of success to many in those days and Johnny enjoyed showing it off. Later in life Johnny was the janitorial superintendent for the North Plainfield, New Jersey High School. Friend was the most gregarious of all of us and had the best personality too. Whenever Friend would come to visit or enter a place where he would see others he knew, his standard expression was always, "Whatze happ-nin," a verbal hello of joyous welcome. Friend became an expert on ball bearings and for many years was in charge of the buying and selling of such equipment for a business in Elizabeth, New Jersey.

The four Avery brothers: Johnny, Friend, Louis, and Jim

Later in Friend's life, he got a call from Roy Schieder, the famed actor who starred in the movie, *Jaws*. Roy said that Friend was an inspiring motivator to him as a teenager when Friend was working at Roy's father's gas station in Cranford. He never forgot the advice and counsel Friend gave him. He honored him by bringing Friend to a school he and Danny Glover, the actor, started in Long Island. He introduced Friend at the school's dedication as the inspiration in his own life. When Friend died, Roy Schieder drove four hours to give the eulogy at Friend's funeral.

My sister and my brothers loved music. Louis played the piano by ear and could not read a note, yet he played beautifully and was one of the best jazz pianists I ever knew. Johnny played the drums, and Friend played the ukulele. The Avery Trio! Friend could have played a guitar by ear as well if he had one. I remember one year they joined with two friends and formed a band and played several times down on Elise Street in what we called the big house. It was a house with a large living room that could be used for dancing. I was too young to go see them but I know they must have had great fun playing for others in the big house in that dimly lit, smoke-filled room with bodies on the dance floor moving in sync with that syncopated rhythm.

After Alice was divorced from Thomas Bauknight, she came back to the house on Johnson Avenue to raise her daughter Roberta. My brother Friend married Sylvia Cox of a well-known black family in Cranford. They had a daughter named Mary, whom we nicknamed Tessie. After they were divorced, Friend brought Mary back to live at 47 Johnson Avenue. Louis and his wife Inez had a child, Sandra, and after the war years also lived in the same house and raised their daughter there. So my mother, Alice, and Inez helped in raising this third generation in this small house my father had built in 1911. My niece, Sandra still lives in the house on Johnson Avenue.

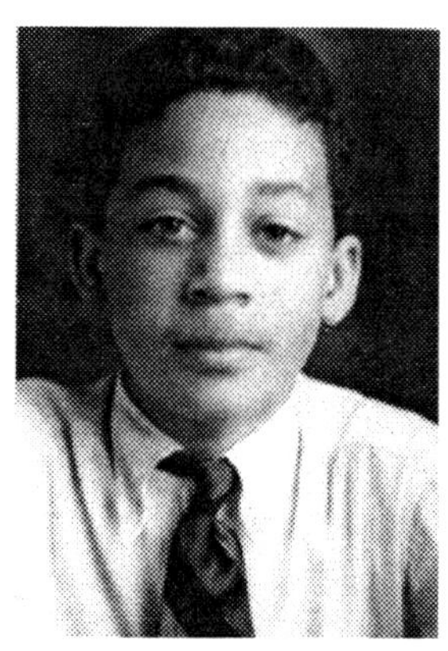

Jim in fifth grade at Sherman Elementary School

I enjoyed going to school and in the fourth and fifth grades fell in love with books. I loved to read about the exploits of the Rover Boys and about Brer Rabbit and other animal stories in the Burgess books. Tom Sawyer and Huck Finn were real to me, too. I ran away with them and felt the trauma they felt during their rafting experience. Many times after school, my fifth grade teacher would ride me in the rumble seat of her car to the library where the books that I read would come to life for me. On June 22, 1934, I received a "Home Reading Certificate" in fifth grade for reading ten books from an approved list, and I still have the certificate signed by Charles A. Wallace, the principal, Cora B. Wakefield, my teacher, Sarah Edmonds, the supervising principal, and May D. Bradley, the librarian.

After-school athletics in the upper elementary grades were great fun too. Our Sherman School teams played the other local schools in touch football and soccer. I don't remember much about competition in basketball or in track. I do remember the fun we had beating Roosevelt School and Lincoln School in soccer and touch football. I will never forget our gym teacher, Mr. Walter J. Coffee, who had us box in gym class. I hated the sessions when Mr. Coffee would match me up with Clifford Schindler, a big ox of a guy, larger than life to me. Clifford would swing those gloves from all directions, his fists whirling like a windmill. He would always out punch me much to Mr. Coffee's sarcastic delight. I guess that is why I never liked to participate in that sport. I grew increasingly competitive as years went by, but I never took my aggressiveness to the point where I lost my cool and ended up in a real fight. Through all my years of life, I have never been in a fight with anyone.

When we were in eighth grade in Sherman School, we were like elders to all the younger kids who looked up to us, probably because we had made it to that point and would soon be going off to the high school. Mrs. Tunner, who later became a principal, was my eighth grade teacher. She was a good one too. I liked science classes with her the best of all, particularly when she taught us about astronomy. One evening our class had to go back to Sherman School to meet with Mrs. Tunner and look at the constellations we were studying in the sky. I remember seeing the Pleiades (the Seven Sisters), Orion the Hunter, and the Big and Little Dippers. Ever since that evening, when I look at the stars, I recognize those constellations and think about that night in Mrs. Tunner's class.

Sherman School is no longer in existence. Where it stood is a large grassy plot of ground used for children's soccer games. The area does not look like it ever held the buildings and the playground that once were there. Two other elementary schools have been built since those days to house the increased number of children who now live in that section of town.

When I was thirteen, weekends and during the summer I played touch football with older boys in the street on Johnson Avenue. There you had to be fast, accurate, and shifty. I am sure that playing with them helped me develop my physical capabilities. My brother Johnny was a big help too. He worked in a store on North Avenue that sold sports equipment, and he got me my first football, baseball glove, bat, and ball that I ever owned. He, above all the other brothers, seemed to be more overtly proud of anything I did athletically.

During the summer in my Junior High years, there was a vacant lot across the street from my house on Johnson Avenue next to the Givens' home where neighbors used to plant corn. It was not unusual at the time for neighbors to use an empty lot on the street to grow food like corn, string beans, and carrots. One particular year no one grew anything on the lot next to the Givens' home. I made a pole-vaulting area there with a runway and a landing pit that included a lot of sand I mixed with the dirt to make it softer to land on. There, with makeshift stiff poles, my best friend Tommy Stevenson and I would practice pole vaulting. Ten feet was as high as I could go and that looked pretty high to me. We did not have a playground in our area. The town apparently did not feel one was necessary. The street was our playground. With pieces of coal, I marked off an oval track on the concrete, and with a stopwatch my brother Johnny gave me, I got the kids in the area to participate in track meets. We even included a long distance race that ran through the woods bordering our street and the Garwood community. I loved to time the various races and record the results. I would challenge the kids like Andrew and Charlie Limone, the Tarver boys, and the Hurtt brothers always to try and better their particular record. Poor and inadequate as the conditions were, this kind of activity enabled me later on in high school to compete not only in pole vaulting and broad jumping, but to win a state hurdling championship. It was also an early sign of my love for teaching and coaching young people.

In our leisure time we built our own scooters, using old wooden crates and three pieces of two-by-four wood. One of the two-by-fours formed the handle on the top of the crate and the other two formed a cross under the bottom of the wooden crate where we could attach the skates we used as runners. We raced our flying machines up and down Johnson Avenue with our foot acting like a rotating propeller, weaving around each other as we went. We played tennis in the street, too, stringing an old net from one pole to another across the street. It was not as if we had a lot of traffic to worry about since there were few cars on Johnson Avenue, and they were not seen for hours at a time. We did everything on that concrete that other kids with more advantages would do on a real playground except ride swings and the seesaw.

The fellows around my age on Johnson Avenue played baseball on a makeshift field up the hill at the end of the street. We used stones for bases and old screening for a partial backstop. I remember that we played the white boys who lived in that part of Garwood that bordered on Johnson Avenue. They had a field just as unkempt as ours. The baseball we used was never new. It was an old taped-up version that had to be refurbished with new black tape often during the game. One of the fields we played on was next to the home of one of the Garwood boys who would get the water we drank from a spigot on the side of his house. He would bring the water back in a milk bottle and all of us, white and black, drank water out of that same milk bottle. Nobody ever thought anything negative about it. It never occurred to us that we were different in any respect that mattered. We were all just poor and innocent of any feelings of race. We never thought about the fact that after all the games, we went our respective ways and never had any other social contact. As we grew older we had even less contact except in organized school sports. No doubt this lessening of contact as we grew older played a subtle part in shaping prejudice and segregation later in life. On the other hand, playing games with each other, in my view, must have also had some kind of positive impact on racial attitudes later in life.

I loved anything that was athletic. It kept me in good shape without worrying about having things to do. In those years,

I never thought about doing anything that would be bad for me. I never smoked or drank liquor. I never touched a cigarette until I was 25 years old and then only smoked cigarettes until I was 31. I never used drugs or knew of anyone who used them or sold them. Drugs were a non-entity. I never heard the word syphilis or gonorrhea until I went into the army in 1942! I was no prude. I knew young people drank and smoked. My brother Friend smoked. Alice did for a while, then stopped. Johnny and Louis never did smoke. As young adults, two of my brothers drank occasionally, but never regularly or in excess. My father smoked cigars. He never drank, nor did my mother. Drugs were never used by any of my family, nor ever really talked about at home. The whole idea of drugs, liquor, or smoking was never a big thing as far as I was concerned.

When I was growing up, the evenings on Johnson Avenue were quiet times. After dinner we would end up on our porches or on the stoop, often with our parents, listening to *Amos and Andy*, *The Green Hornet*, and *The Shadow* before Gabriel Heater came on with the seven o'clock news. The news then seemed to be only the very important current events. With no air conditioning, those porches particularly in the early evening were meeting places for family and friends. People often sat on their porches until well after dark.

I remember when Joe Louis fought in his heavyweight championship boxing matches that people in the neighborhood listened to these bouts, often on the porches. When he won with a knockout, people would run out into the street cheering and banging pots and pans. Mr. Barnes, who lived directly across the street from our house, would shoot his revolver up in the air as if to put a happy resounding bang on the celebration. All of us took pride in what Joe Louis did. After all, he was of our race, and he was a winner over all obstacles. It was like Jesse Owens, the great track and field star, winning records in the 1936 Olympics over in Germany. We were proud when he won those Olympic events and proved his expertise in track and field, disproving the racial superiority that Hitler was preaching.

Later in life, I got to know Jesse Owens very well. I first met him in Chicago, Illinois, when I went there to meet with black leadership to get their assistance in increasing the number of blacks operating our service stations. Jesse was a partner in an Owens-West promotional firm. They ran a weekly program where mostly women would gather, have a light breakfast and win prizes and get souvenirs. I last saw Jesse when I visited him in his private office in Phoenix, Arizona, in 1976. I cherish the picture he autographed for me with warm personal comments.

Going back to my youth, many a night, my buddy Steve and I would sit on the cement curb out by our homes solving the problems of our little world. I remember too, one evening while we were sitting there, that another friend James Charles walked passed us up the hill to a wooded area with a young girl that I thought was my girlfriend. Man, was I heart broken! I decided that I would never speak to her again in life. My buddy Tommy seemed to share my grief agreeing with me on the pledge that I had made. Of course, I soon forgot the pledge. We talked about the things we would do when we got older. We let our imaginations run rampant. Even now, some 75 years later, we still talk about those days when our imagination predicted the future.

Saturday afternoons were great days for going to the movies. I seldom had the money. My buddy, Steve, would get enough from the coins that would fall out of his father's pocket when his dad fell asleep in the living room chair to pay for both of us. I loved it when we would see cowboy movies with Tom Mix or Hopalong Cassidy and Hoot Gibson. Westerns were my favorite movies then, and they still are today. I liked the slapstick comedy of Laurel and Hardy and Joe E. Brown, too. Saturdays, the Cranford motion picture theater offered two features and a cartoon, a great value for our 15-cent ticket! Funny some of the things we remember. One winter day when all of us on the street went to see the movie *Frankenstein*, it was dark when we came out of the theater. "Frankenstein" seemed to lurk in every shadow. All someone had to do was to feign a scream, and we would scatter like leaves in the wind. We were scared to death all the way home after movies like that. The next day we would laugh about our fears.

The people on the street where I lived had some of the greatest lawn parties with the tastiest food. Some families, like my own, used colorful Japanese lanterns to light the lawn area and adorned the tables with colorful paper tablecloths on which they put succulent dishes like fried chicken, macaroni and cheese, yams, Parker House rolls, and string beans cooked with ham hocks. The deserts like sweet potato, rhubarb, peach, and apple pies and sometime homemade ice cream were simply to die for.

The music, syncopated jazz, came from a 78-rpm record player or the radio. The area always had the appearance of a very festive miniature carnival where neighbors and friends just enjoyed each other's company, ate the succulent food, and carried on their jovial conversations over all the laughter and sounds of syncopated jazz until well after dark.

Those were wonderful years. Sunday was a day of rest and a day of church attendance. We wore our best clothes on Sunday, because of Sunday school and church service. It was like a strange parade on Sunday to see us kids walking en masse from Johnson Avenue down town to High Street where the black churches were located. And, if one noticed it, they would see a black Studebaker patrolling along with the group. That was Deacon Tucker riding slowly with Mrs. Tucker sitting regally in the back seat making sure that their grand kids behaved as they walked with the group to church. In those days it was a normal, well-accepted thing to dress up on Sunday and go to Sunday School. No one ever questioned it. On the way home, those with a few cents would stop at Rickters corner store for assorted pieces of candy.

What Mrs. Tucker never knew was that when she and Deacon Tucker left for Wednesday night Prayer Meeting, I would sneak into the side door of their house and sit for almost an hour on the cellar stairs with their granddaughter Carolyn Daniels. I was 15 years old at the time and had a boyish crush on Carolyn. I was so naive that in reflection I was just stupid. I never tried to kiss her or even hold her close on those cellar stairs. Deacon Tucker and Mrs. Tucker had nothing to worry about with dumb me on the scene.

The two churches that the kids on the street attended on Sunday were both on High Street and not too far from each other. One was the African Methodist Episcopal Church and the other was the First Baptist Church. The Baptist Church was the older having been built in the 1897. As I reflect, I think it was attending Sunday school that in some indescribable way helped strengthen my sense of right and wrong and good and bad. Like most church Sunday schools, the lessons we were taught centered on those parts of the scripture that the teachers could relate to like honesty, vanity, selfishness, and faith. Each year, we performed at special Easter and Christmas children's programs. When you were young like that you did not fully understand the wonderful things you were learning. You sort of got it by osmosis. You didn't realize that you were getting a moral foundation that would impact your way of life forever.

Winter times in those days seemed to have more snow than we see today. And it seemed to last longer too. We had great fun on Saturdays when we went down to the frozen pond by Elise Street across South Avenue and played hockey all day. We made makeshift hockey sticks and used cubed-shaped stones for pucks. It was something awesome when some kids finally got real hockey sticks, a real puck, and ice skates. We made a fire to warm our hands. Sometimes we would dash home to get a quick sandwich and come back to continue the game. We never seemed to get tired, perhaps a little cold late in the day, but never tired.

Many of us had sleds like those made by the American Flyers and Zephyr sled companies that were used up and down Johnson Avenue, particularly after the snow got smooth and icy. Most of the sleds were not new and some of them were held together by strong twine. We kept the sled runners shiny and slick by filing them all the time. The most fun with the sleds was when we took them down to High Street with its high and long hill. Everyone flocked to High Street when there was a heavy snow and had the greatest fun sleigh riding down the hill. It was particularly good fun to belly-whop on some sled or jump on top of another person, sometimes on a girl, and enjoy the great ride downhill! Winters and snow-covered hills are magical when you are a kid.

Of all the seasons, however, fall was the one that had the most distinctive sounds, sights, smells, and fragrances. I am thinking of the brilliance of the red, yellow, and orange colors that adorned the trees and special bushes. And when those leaves had fallen from the trees and been raked into piles, we could dive into them as if we were jumping into a pile of feathers. I remember the fragrance of those leaves that wafted lightly through the air as they were burned. Funny, though, you could easily tell if you had been standing near the burning leaves because your clothes would absorb an acrid odor different from what you would smell from a distance. Those of us who stood too close reeked of that acrid smell and the only recourse was to go home, remove the clothes, and take a bath. Then there was something else that was wonderful about the fall season. It was the sound of cheering football crowds and the playing of the Notre Dame University fight song that Cranford adopted for its football games. I just loved that time of year. It is too bad that it all ended with bare trees, weather with an increasing chill and a feeling of things going into hibernation. But, one could always think ahead. I always remembered the poet Shelley's words, when he said: "If winter comes, can spring be far behind?"

IV

High School Years

The high school football games in Cranford were played on West End Avenue on a football field called the Oval. When I was in eighth grade, I remember going up to the Oval on Saturday afternoons and sneaking in under the fence to watch Cranford High play football against other towns. I can still visualize Cy Dadd, a fine quarterback, Frank Nordstrom and Joe Klein as good running backs, and Howard Stanley, who was a great kicker. Howard went on to Princeton where he captained the team as a senior. I enjoyed watching those fellows. Funny, I could not tell you now if Cranford won or lost the games I sneaked in to see. I only knew that one day I wanted to be out on that field running, throwing, and kicking that football too! I never got to play on that historic old Oval. In 1936, the town broke ground there to build a new high school and the high school games for a number of years after that were played on a field on Walnut Avenue.

I was promoted to the ninth grade in 1937 and spent that year in Cleveland School, a building converted from a grammar school to a temporary high school. The high school was finished in 1939 when I was a sophomore and our classes were moved into the new building on West End Avenue. Naturally, I went out for varsity football that year. The coach was Coach J. Seth Weekly. Coach Weekly was part American Indian. He was born in Alabama and went to school there. Seth, as we often called him out of his presence, never lost his southern drawl. He was old-fashioned in many ways and was ultra conservative and not at all innovative. He was a frugal man too and did not push the administration to replace the old and outdated uniforms we used which were as old-fashioned and conservative as he.

The jerseys were very plain and of a cheap quality. The football pants had a drab brown color and were loosely fit. He taught the single wing offense and never tried new formations like the Wing T with one back behind the center. At that time, he coached three sports, football, basketball, and track, and did so with the same old-fashioned demeanor. Mr. Walter Coffee, the man who had been my elementary gym teacher, was the baseball coach and an elementary school administrator. It was not until 1939 that Cranford brought on another person, Ben Carnavale, a former NYU all-star, to coach basketball. Ben was one of the finest coaches I ever knew.

Practicing my passing skills at Cranford High, 1939

I made the varsity football team that sophomore year and was the starting tailback in Weekly's single wing offence. Needless to say, I was in heaven every time I ran out on that football field. Those years of playing street football on Johnson Avenue were about to pay off. Sophomore year was the beginning of a period that would change the course of my life. Playing football in high school was a very natural thing to me, like breathing and walking. I had an inner sense of confidence and when I ran through or around the line with the ball, I just knew I was going to be very difficult to tackle. When I threw a pass, I knew how to throw it to the right spot. And when I kicked the ball, I loved to make it spiral high into the air.

Honing my running skills before a big game

During each of the three years in senior high school I played first-string halfback in J. Seth Weekley's single wing offense. We started our season against East Orange High, a Group Four powerhouse. Cranford, because of its smaller student body, was a Group Two school. Each time we played East Orange they were extremely hard fought games. In 1939 they beat us with a safety made on the fourth play of the game. When I was a senior, the score was 0 to 0. The *Elizabeth Daily Journal* reported that game as follows:

> Avery was in mid-season form as a quarterback and as a safety executing offensive and defensive operations with equal agility. Had either (Cleve) Muldrow or (Sid) Scott been better pass receivers the game might have ended differently, for some of Avery's tosses left little to be desired. (Both dropped forward passes to them as they stood on the opponent's goal line.)

We always played East Orange tough and each year felt we were winners when the score against that bigger team was close.

My first touchdown as a sophomore was against Bernardsville High School whom we beat 13–6. I remember we beat them 12–0 when I was a junior, and I scored one of the touchdowns. Butler High was another school we played each year and did well against. I scored both touchdowns to beat them 14–6 when I was a sophomore. We tied Dover 6 to 6 in 1939 and beat a tough Boundbrook High team 7–6. Our team always played hard-nosed football against other teams, especially like Rahway and Hillside, tying them, beating, or losing to them by one or a few points. Coach Weekley must have been a masochist because he not only arranged games with three Group Four schools, East Orange, Orange and Thomas Jefferson High of Elizabeth, but with several Group Three Schools as well. As I mentioned, we were a Group Two school because of the smaller number of students. If we had played all the games with teams in our own school size, we would have been undefeated all the time!

My senior year in Cranford High School was probably my best. I played particularly well against East Orange in that 0-0 game. I played very well against Roselle whom we beat 27–13, against Dover whom we beat 7–0, and against Bernardsville whom we beat 13–6. Reporting on the next game we had with Rahway High, *The Elizabeth Daily Journal* wrote:

> Cranford's Avery continues to rank as a fine running back, in spite of the fact that Rahway bottled him up. The Rahway punts were kept away from him as much as possible, and on other occasions a guard, Joe Angelo, was sacrificed as a blocker and sent downfield with the ends to good effect. This trio had Avery tied down on every kick. But from scrimmage, the colored quarterback ripped and tore through the Rahway line for plenty of yardage and that Cranford piled up eight first downs to Rahway's seven was largely the result of his hard running, often without adequate blocking or interference.

I got hit on the side of my right leg in the third quarter of that Rahway game that caused the tearing of cartilages on the inside and outside sections of my right knee. Coach Weekly sent me back into that game after my knee was injured because he needed me to call the signals. (Years later, on his last visit to Cranford before he died, he told me he came back especially to apologize to me for using me in games the rest of the season and not giving my leg a chance to heal properly. I told him that playing was my decision. I loved the sport and the team, and I wanted to be out on that field regardless. I urged him not to feel responsible for the injury that I sustained.) As it happened, Rahway High beat us 12-0, but the score might have been different if not for that injury to my right knee. Coach Weekly took me into New York City to a physical therapist to help me exercise and get the knee into some kind of condition so that I could at least walk on it. But, the knee really needed an operation, not just therapy. From that time on I was in quite a bit of pain every day.

While that debilitating injury might have stopped some players from playing football for the rest of the season, blinded by loyalty to my coach and an all-consuming love for the game, I played the remaining games with my right leg heavily tapped from my ankle to my upper thigh. They taped the leg that way to keep it from as much danger as possible. We lost to Hillside 7-6 partly because I could not run through the holes the players made for me. Unfortunately, Cleve Muldrow dropped two of my passes when he was on the goal line, one hitting the number on the front of his jersey! It was another one point game we should have won. In fact, during my three years of varsity football there were seven games we would have won if we had had a good place kicker and if our ends had had sure hands. We lost the next game 13-6 against Group 4 Orange High. We won the following game against Bound Brook, 13-6. My last high school game was the Thanksgiving game against the Group 4 powerhouse Thomas Jefferson whom we upset 19-7.

In covering the game, the major paper in the area, the *Elizabeth Daily Journal* said:

> Typical of a struggle that ensues when a "giant" meets a "small fellow," Cranford outsmarted, outplayed and outran the lumbering Jeffs. Led by Jim Avery, as good a candidate for all-state honors as you ever saw, the Blue and Gold passed and plunged its way to three touchdowns. Without taking any credit away from any member of the squad, Avery was without any doubt the best man on the field that day. The fleet quarterback was all over the playing field, making impossible stops, spectacular runs and heaving bullet-like passes. Once he galloped across the goal himself. Without his effort the game might conceivably have had a different ending.

That year, 1940, I made the New Jersey Scholastic Football Honor Roll. Among all high schools (All Groups) I was chosen the second best quarterback in the state and the First Team quarterback for all the Group Two schools.

I give my mother a great deal of credit for whatever I was in life and for whatever I did athletically. Every week she would make sure that I had good meals with fresh vegetables from Dreyer's Farm on Springfield Avenue. She attended many of the home games too. People told me that there were times when they saw my mother running down the sidelines when I was running down the field toward the goal line. She encouraged me all the time and was always a great supporter of the things I did. I believe that my extra-curricular activities and my good grades along with the achievements in sports gave her great happiness and pride. I know she was extremely proud of my achievements in high school, especially my being president of the school's Student Council in my senior year. After all, I was the baby boy she had late in life, and I was on the way to realizing her dreams.

It was during the basketball season on February 4, 1941, that something occurred that scarred my life forever. When I left home that morning, my mother was in bed, sick. I remember telling her that I loved her and would see her after school and that she would be all right and that God would take care of her. I was coming home that evening after a game we won against Plainfield High School and was walking up Johnson Avenue whistling. When I got to the house before ours I saw our neighbor Gertrude Townsend and I said happily, "Hi, Gertrude!" And, she said to me "Jimmy, don't you know?" That was all she had to say to me. A world full of dread fell down over me. I ran like the wind to our house and met my brother Friend at the door only to learn that Mother had died that evening. In a state of deep shock beyond comprehension, I ran across the street to my friend Tommy Stevenson's house and stayed there in a small room for what seemed like three days. Even though I attended my mother's funeral, to this day, I do not remember the funeral or any of the activities related to my mother's death. I learned my mother had some form of hyperthyroidism and her death was caused by medical treatment to remove the goiter that she had on the side of her neck. The goiter had been there for years. Later I learned that cancer had set in and had begun to restrict breathing and swallowing. Maybe the cobalt treatment hastened her death. It was unfortunate that medical science had not advanced sufficiently at that time to give doctors a better understanding of what to do about growths in the thyroid gland.

The outpouring of love, letters, cards, and comments from fellow students, friends, and Cranford people in general was overwhelming. My mother was just a great lady and everybody seemed to know it. I still think of her very often and wished she knew of the remaining good things that would happen to me in my life. I always wanted her to be proud of me. I knew that she felt I was her last hope, the last of her children to get a good education and to have things in life she could not provide. The pain of her death has never left me. The loss of my mother was so intense within my soul that unconsciously I started to insulate myself from ever having to experience that kind of agony again. It definitely changed how I reacted to potentially traumatic situations. I became more removed and distant on one hand and on the other, I strove to succeed in everything to honor the dreams of my mother.

While life seemed to drain out of me when my mother died, my father maintained a quiet dignified strength and never openly showed his tears to me. In so many senses of the word, my father, throughout his life, seemed to manifest the kind of philosophy founded by the Greek philosopher Zeno, who was a stoic. Zeno taught, as Webster's Dictionary states it, that men should be "free from passion, unmoved by joy or grief and submit without complaint to unavoidable necessity." I cannot say my dad was a complete stoic because there were times that events and comments brought sounds of laughter and expressions of pride from him. But on occasions of sadness and suffering, he seemed to keep his feelings safely buried and the aches and pains they caused were undisclosed to people around him.

It took me several weeks after my mother's death before I could once again focus on athletics fully, but I was soon back in competitive activity. While I was not a great basketball player and was still wearing a brace on my knee, I was a starter on the team and later in March of 1941 helped to win the Sectional State Championship. I loved playing basketball with fellow students like the great Joe Duff, Dave Sterrett, and Cleve Muldrow. Joe was a rather diminutive fellow, but he was a true All-State player. Later in life, Joe Duff became the head baseball coach for the United States Naval Academy. Ben Carnevale, a former NYU basketball star, was a great coach and had a lot to do with our being a winning team. (During World War II, Ben coached the University of North Carolina Pre-Flight group. After the war he coached at the US Naval Academy.) We missed becoming County Champs in that senior year when we played Johnson Regional, losing by a basket in sudden death overtime. That was one of the saddest nights I ever had as a high school player of any sport.

I played three sports in high school, football, basketball, and track. In my senior year, I won the State Group II, 220 yards Low Hurdling Championship with a brace on my right knee. In the dual meets, I also broad jumped, threw the discus, and pole-vaulted, all with that brace on my leg. I scored a lot of points for our track team, but I did the best in the low hurdles. I was not a good quarter mile runner and therefore never ran in the very popular Penn Relays held annually in April at the University of Pennsylvania in Philadelphia. I could run very well for 220 yards, half way around the oval track, but after that I seem to run out of gas like a car that had used its last drop of energy.

Number 7 on Cranford High's Group II Sectional Basketball Championship Team, 1941

I did not spend all my leisure time with sports. Like most boys I, too, grew to know that there were girls in the world. I had a steady girlfriend during my senior high years. Her name was Mary Ella Brooks, and she lived down the street in the flats where my mother had forbid me to go when I was a child. Mary had the greatest personality, always smiling, always a happy person. While my mother never really knew it, I walked Mary home after school many days, saw her when we went to the movies, and some times on Sundays after church. Mary and I were a twosome until World War II. At one point during my military service, we talked about getting married. Somehow that never came to be. I will never forget the day just after I started dating Mary, I stopped by her home and her mother was standing on the porch. She came up to me, looked me in the eye and said: "Mary thinks you are a nice boy, and I hope I will always be able to say the same thing." Needless to say,

I never forgot what she said and every time the necking got heavy, her veiled comment brought a deep chill to my bones and threw cold water on my emotions. As we got older, Mary Ella and I often talked of marriage but, somehow, we never got to the point of doing anything about it. Mary Ella and I are still friends after all these years, although I don't see Mary and her husband except on some unusual occasion like someone's funeral.

My Cranford High School graduation picture, June 1941

During my high school years, while sports took a great deal of my time, I was very much involved in other extra-curricular activities. While I was a senior, I was elected by the students to be "Mayor" of Cranford during the Youth Week activities sponsored by the Rotary Club in the Spring of 1941. I had to conduct the weekly Rotary Club meeting, the Lions Club meeting and a meeting of the Township Committee, as well as help run several Youth Week events. My "committee-men," who were also elected by the student body, were Jim Harford, "police commissioner"; Scoville Hager, "fire commissioner"; Robert Winkle "finance commissioner"; David Sterrett, "road commissioner"; and Norman Aurand, "township clerk." We actually met with township officials to learn the proper procedures at committee meetings before we convened the meeting to review township activity and to transact necessary municipal business.

Chronicle

James Avery Elected 'Mayor' of Youth Week

Fishing Competition Saturday; Treasure Hunt This Afternoon

James Avery

V

Hail Columbia

I was very fortunate to have several male teachers who had attended Columbia College and had a keen interest in getting good athletes who were capable students to go there. They never stopped encouraging me to keep my grades up and to keep doing the very best I could in all of my school activities. It paid off for me. In the spring of 1941, I received one of the two scholarships awarded to Union County students on the basis of scholarly achievement to go to Columbia College, Columbia University. This was a $300 Charles Sterling Hayden Memorial Scholarship granted by the Columbia University's Faculty Committee on Scholarships. Without that scholarship I never could have gone to Columbia College. The $300 paid for my tuition. As a scholarship holder, I was eligible for what was known as a Group I room that was priced at $150 for the year. When I arrived at Columbia in September, I received the National Youth Administration (NYA) job and a meal job to take care of other needs and expenses. The meal job I had was great. I was in charge of the breakfast fruit and juice section. Man, I loved that job! I roomed with George Hudanish, the fellow who got the other scholarship in Union County. He was from Roselle Park. Cranford was well represented in my dorm that year because Horace Potter, a high school graduate in 1939, and Harold Brod, a classmate of mine in 1941, were there also.

Before I knew about the scholarship to Columbia College, the coach of Morris Brown College in Atlanta, Georgia, wanted me to go to school there as did the coach of Johnson C. Smith College. There was also a Dr. Longshore, a dentist from East Orange, New Jersey, who was involved in a program at the YMCA in that city that recognized outstanding black athletes in New Jersey. He was a Lincoln University graduate and wanted me to attend that school on a scholarship. (How ironic that 51 years later, I was elected to be a Trustee on the Lincoln University Board of Trustees.)

While I was a freshman at Columbia, I wrote back to the Alumni Editor of the local paper to tell about life at one of the finest universities in the entire world. One of the paragraphs of that letter went like this:

> Columbia, as many of you think, isn't located in the heart of this bustling city, but is placed atop Morningside Heights. Its many buildings are large and majestic and seem to boast about the greatness of the school. Just like every other Columbian, I, too, feel the great responsibility of living up to the high standards of the university.

I also wrote about some of the harmless shenanigans that went on in the dormitories.

I went out for football, basketball, and track in my freshman year at college. I was the starting halfback for the freshman football team, a starting guard on the basketball team, and a low hurdler on the track team. Low hurdling was my best event. As I had mentioned, I had won the NJ State Group II championship and frankly felt I was pretty good at it. When I was a freshman, I represented Columbia College in the low hurdles in the New York Metropolitan Meet at Randalls Island, a meet of all the colleges in the metropolitan area. I placed second. The winner was a fellow from NYU named "Moon" Munshein who later became the decathlon champion in the World Olympics. While I wanted desperately to win, I felt more at ease knowing that it took an Olympic winner to beat me.

I loved running track. During the winter of 1941, I often practiced with one of the great Olympic quarter milers. He was Johnny Borican, who lived in Bridgeton, New Jersey, and had attended the University of Pittsburgh for his undergraduate work. Johnny loved to train on the wooden track that was set up on South Field outside of Butler Library and would use my room to change into running gear whenever he practiced at Columbia. Johnny Borican won the United States Decathlon and Pentathlon titles, an unheard of feat of athletic greatness. At the time I was not aware of the membership or the activities of the Omega Psi Phi Fraternity. There were no minority fraternities at Colombia at that time. Much to my amazement later in life I learned that Johnny Borican was then a member of the Omega Psi Phi Fraternity, an organization that was to play a great part in my future.

Being at Columbia was a very different experience. Everything appeared to be huge, the dorms were majestic, the Butler Library massive, and the statue of Alma Mater sat regally in front of the domed Seth Low administration building, which is still the centerpiece of the many large, imposing buildings. You just knew that you were at Columbia College for one reason: to learn, learn, learn. There were few blacks in Columbia College during that time. Several of them were African tribal princes, sent over by their fathers to prepare them for future leadership. Race was not a factor of concern, at least I never felt that it was. The white students were there to learn too, and it was evident that at Columbia having a broad, inquisitive view of life and living seemed to be the prevailing sentiment.

In my sophomore year I went out for the varsity football team. The *Elizabeth Daily Journal* had a very flattering article announcing this fact.

CRANFORD'S AVERY AMONG SOPH STARS AT COLUMBIA

> Jim Avery, the Negro halfback who was rated one of Union County's two or three best ball carriers in 1940 when he ripped up opposition for Cranford High is now part of a rather pleasant "headache" for Coach Lou Little at Columbia. The keeper of the lions is trying to decide how to fit a group of sophomore stars, including Avery, into the Columbia varsity.
>
> Avery sparkled with the better than average Columbia freshman team a year ago, and after a week of drilling with the varsity squad this season he was rated in the university's football pamphlet as one of the "outstanding sophomore candidates."

JERSEY BOYS ADD STRENGTH TO COLUMBIA

I thoroughly enjoyed playing for one of the great coaches in America, Lou Little. He was a very hard taskmaster. I remember one practice when he thought that I did not carry out the play as well as I should have. I was in the huddle after that play when I felt a foot in my rear that sent me over the center's head, a boot in the tail that coincided with a "get off your ass going through that line if you are going to play for me!" The backfield coach, Cliff Battle, once a great player himself, later put his arm around me and said, "Jim, he would not have done that unless he really liked you!" I did better after that, though I felt that it was a strange way for Coach Little to display affection.

It was just before the game with Cornell University that I expected to have a lot of playing time when I was severely injured in a scrimmage against Manhattan College. My right knee that I had injured when I was a senior in high school received a blow that tore the cartilage on the inside and outer side and ended my athletic activity for that year. Several months later I had the knee operated on at the Columbia Presbyterian Hospital.

Social life was not a big factor for me at Columbia at this time. My schedule was just too tight. With a meal job in early morning followed by classes, an NYA job, and sports practice in the afternoon until past dark, then the training table for dinner and back to my room to study before going to bed around 11:00 P.M., I did have a chance for some social activity on the weekends. The results, however, were rather mixed.

One Saturday, when I was still a freshman and a small town guy, a fellow student, Jimmy Thomas, a good looking sophisticated guy who was a part of the high society among blacks in the New York area, asked me to go out on a double date with him. My date was Betty Pougue, who happened to be Miss Howard University for 1941. She was so beautiful. I kept saying to myself, my Lord she is gorgeous! I think my friend Jimmy Thomas had built me up as a football star. I was such a green horn that all I did after Jimmy parked the car in some wooded area was to gawk at her and make idle conversation. I felt I was being a gentleman, too. All this idle talking about nothing special was going on while Jimmy Thomas and his date were literally out of sight up in the front seat. The next day Jimmy told me that Betty Pougue told him never to bring "that shy, do-nothing guy around again!" I was so naive.

How stupid I was about the black middle-class social life that existed at the time. I was not aware of an existing phenomenon in black society. There was a middle-upper class group, largely light skinned, whose parents were all college graduates, many were doctors and lawyers whose children were members of social groups like the Jack and Jill. Their parents were also in organizations like the Links and the Nordsmen. Most of the children in this social caste always went to the same summer camp and were very cliquish in their social life. Here I was a small time kid, not knowledgeable about this kind of society, out on a date with members of this middle-upper class societal group that had all the characteristics of white society. (These organizations still play a significant and highly respected role in the social life of Black America.) Jimmy Thomas introduced me to this group in what ended up being a very uncomfortable experience for me. Jimmy Thomas later became a successful pediatrician in New York City.

Everything about my social life up to that point had no relevance to this element of higher society except that I was light skinned with blue eyes. It was then that I began to learn about the caste system among blacks in America.

Later in the year I met another beautiful and talented young black lady named Margaret Johnson. She lived with her mother, sister, and stepfather, who was a doctor on 138th Street in Harlem. She was a student at Radcliffe. I don't remember the details of how I met her. It was probably a social event where college kids got together at Columbia. Anyway, Margaret Johnson and I developed a warm, platonic relationship during the summer of 1942. I think her mother really liked me and encouraged me to go with her daughter. I am sure that being a Columbia College student was a plus factor too. There were a number of occasions during that summer when I called

Margaret on a Sunday afternoon from my home in Cranford, New Jersey, and she would tell me to come over for dinner and that her mother would hold dinner until I got there. I would put on my only suit, take the train to Jersey City, cross the Hudson on the ferry, and take the subway up to 135th Street and walk over to their home on 138th street. Sure enough, they would be waiting for me to arrive before having dinner. Margaret Johnson was a fine person and a brilliant lady. She ended up teaching Mathematics at Hunter College. I lost touch after I went into the military service. Somehow, maybe because I had grown up in a different social setting, I never felt compelled to be an active part of that middle-upper class group of blacks that played off each other for the social togetherness they felt was important to them.

VI

Military Service

America went to war against Japan and Germany in 1941. In late 1941, many of the football players went down to join the Marine Corps, hoping to become officer candidates. Naturally, even though I was the only black on the team, I went too. I took the physical and believe it or not, the knee that was injured stood up under the examination. Yet the Marines turned me down saying my feet were too flat for the amount of activity that would be required of me. To me, it was a decision based upon prejudice. It was the first time I had ever really recognized and felt the impact of real prejudice. The truth of the matter was they were not looking for any blacks to become Marine officers at that time. I felt that I was being discriminated against on the false pretense of having flat feet! I was deeply angered. The Marine Corps just did not want a black fellow to be taken in as a part of this white group. Despite that belittling situation with the Marines, I still wanted to join the army, so in early 1942, I went down to 90 Church Street in New York and enlisted in what was known as the Enlisted Reserve Corps (ERC). My serial number was #12194505 and that was the number on my dog tag too. While the other guys in the Marines and Air Force were called up to join the service, those of us who enlisted in the ERC were allowed to continue with our schooling until called up for active duty in May of 1943. I was happy that I was able to complete my sophomore year's studies before being called up for active military service.

I enlisted because my brothers had been called for active military service, and I really wanted to do just as they had done. I must admit, though, that I had some unstated misgivings. When I enlisted, I knew I was joining a segregated army. I knew I was joining other young black men to fight in a segregated unit for things that we couldn't have: rights and freedom of living and going any place we wanted to go in America. I wondered, at the time, if the war would help us achieve these ends or if the war would end with blacks further behind in political and social-economic conditions than ever before. I never expressed those thoughts openly until later in life. I was always within the parameters of what was apparently right to do or say. I was a get-along-with kind of guy; however, I never thought I lacked the courage to speak out. I liked being in the spotlight but only with things I liked to do and was successful doing.

Well, I got the notice! The United States Army had finally added to its ranks a new and potentially industrious soldier. I remember the document that came in the mail, it read, "Private James Stephen Avery report to the Reception Center at Fort Dix, New Jersey, for active duty, May 8, 1943." That day arrived, and I went on to Fort Dix wondering and pretending, anxious but yet skeptical about beginning a new experience. My pretentiousness and doubtful nature was the result of three things: my upbringing, what I wanted out of life, and how I felt about people in general. It seems that people entering an endeavor like this are caught between strong and conflicting desires. Broadly speaking, they are love of home life with its various offshoots; and secondly, an unfounded desire for experiences not knowing how those experiences would turn out.

As I departed from home going to report for active duty, I said my goodbyes to everyone and listened respectfully with tense nerves to my father, who said, "Just remember you are a man, unafraid and daring, make the best of it. Don't ever get to the place where you won't pray. Be a good chap and take care of yourself." With clouded eyes, firm clasps of hands, he kissed my cheeks, and we parted. He tried his best to withhold his disrupted composure and outwardly he did. But underneath I knew he was disturbed and worried even though I was a man. After all, I was his youngest son and his fourth to enter the military service of our country.

In the induction room at Fort Dix Military Base in New Jersey, I was separated in a very obvious manner from my white comrades and ushered to a barracks where I would be among members of my own race. I was fully aware that this would happen but it still disturbed me a great deal. I had been raised on a street that was racially diverse, and I had participated in school life in high school and college in ways that had no impact on race. And while I knew about housing segregation, church segregation, and the like, I still didn't like it when it came to serving my country. What a great opportunity the various service units of our country had to prove, by mixing racial groups, that people can live together, work together, play together, and grow increasingly to respect each other and to achieve important goals together. (Later in life, a good friend and fraternity brother of mine, Attorney Grant Reynolds, a very prominent person in civic and political life in the 40s in New York State, told me that he and A. Phillip Randolph, who was head of the RR Pullman Porters Union at the time, were instrumental in persuading President Truman to integrate the Armed Forces.)

The activity of chief interest and significance in the induction area were the examinations. The exams were three in number. One was an IQ exam composed of vocabulary and arithmetic questions to test one's mental brightness. The second was a Morse code test to find out how good a person could comprehend signal sound relationships by ear. The third was a mechanical aptitude exam. It was composed of common sense answers concerning everyday mechanical phenomena. I left the classification center triumphant yet secretly skeptical of a few problems that I answered rather dubiously.

After lunch I went to take another physical exam. I had to undergo this test because I had had an operation on my knee to remove the damaged cartilage since the time of my enlistment. I passed with flying colors and fell into the general routine of reception center activities with a new and reinvigorated feeling about things.

We received our inoculations—the needles—the same day, getting one that was known as the "hook." It was a tetanus shot. The effects were astounding. After taking five steps I felt as if I had received an overdose of acid in my arm. It burned and throbbed and ached for many hours and for a time it was hard to raise my right arm. After that, in later years, when we were given such inoculations, I dreaded receiving the hook. After the needles, we were marched by counter after counter getting articles of clothing. Some that we knew would fit and others that we knew would not. Anyway, filled with arm pain and misfit clothing I pushed my way outside, fully aware that now I really was a soldier in this man's army.

During the return march back to our camp area, my whole civilian life passed through my mind. I saw my youth and my growing love for aggressive ways. I saw myself as Student Council President at Cranford High and the successful winding of my way along the road of high school sports. I saw myself entering Columbia College, Columbia University, and lastly I saw myself leaving college for the army, interrupting a life pattern that was now doubtful of completion. All I could hope for was the best of success under God's guidance here in the army. I was now a part of a new life and I could not help but realize that while I once controlled my own destiny, my immediate future would be based upon someone else's decisions.

That night, I went to the service club where a group of stage artists from Newark, New Jersey, entertained us royally. I had a lot of respect for that group, not because of what they presented, but for the fact that they seemed to genuinely enjoy entertaining us. The next day I spent cleaning out guns. It was a job that at the time held a lot of significance, for I learned the various parts of the principle gun the military soldier used in fighting the war. We had been told that eventually we would be shipped to an infantry unit where rifles and shooting apparatus would be a vital part of our everyday living.

One day, my comrades Jim Moss and Arron Biddle and I got together on a deep discussion on racial matters and how the black man should progress. Jim Moss was strongly class conscious. He believed in the black man guiding himself by his own efforts and when he finds an opportunity such as the war today, he should move ahead and demand things he wanted. I opposed him on this point because I felt that strong militant action on the part of blacks would not work in the long term.

Nevertheless, Moss clung to his views, emphasizing his belief that the masses of people cannot refute the desire of a people who show their qualifications and press strongly against the ropes of oppression. Arron's thoughts were based upon self-improvement. He felt that the black man could never get ahead in life until he removed the obstacles planted by his own misgivings. In that way he believed that the black man would be preparing himself for progress and that he would not be denied new opportunities or lose the gains made. My thoughts were a composite of characteristics built by self-observation and incorporated some of the things Arron was saying. I firmly believed that blacks had moved an amazing distance since getting freedom in 1860s. I felt that their attitude about subordination and prejudice worked in favor of perpetuating the evils. I felt that the black man should remove some of those scars and attempt to break down the white man's prejudicial feelings by showing that he can act just as intelligently, accept just as many responsibilities, do the job just as effectively, and move on to higher and higher achievements, just like anyone else. Only after a revolutionary systematized development in education, in economic life, and in politics can the black race secure its desires and be a real part of the American dream.

That night Arron Biddle and I slept in the supply room where we voiced more of our opinions on different customs and traditions of present-day life. Once again our similarities came forth and once again we reminded ourselves of our intended get-together on our first furlough. At 3:30 A.M. the next morning our plans were all but shattered when a soldier yelled into the supply room, "Get up Avery and Biddle, you're both being shipped out!"

It was not long before I was dressed in the olive garb and standing at parade rest with other soldiers, all with packed barracks bags beside us. We were going west. That was all I knew. When we got down to the shipping and receiving department, all they told us was that we would go through Chicago and end up in any one of the many states west of Illinois.

Well, looking like the characters of Chaucer's famous *Canterbury Tales*, we left Fort Dix behind. It was difficult to describe the way many of us felt when the bus pulled away.

We were glad because we wanted to hurry up and find out where we were going and what we were expected to do. Many of us wanted to begin our basic training and get ratings and maybe go to OCS. Then, again, in a way we didn't want to go for we were about to have a chance to go home for a visit. At all costs, we were a bunch of confused human beings, our brains a mass of conflicting thoughts. We had a touch of good luck when we got to the station and the Sergeant in charge gave us a careless hint as to our destination. He very casually mentioned St. Louis, Missouri, as the length of our train ride. To me that meant we were heading for a base not too far from that mid-western city.

At the railroad terminal in Trenton, the Sergeant proved to be a good sport and let us call home. I raced upstairs, excited at having the chance to surprise my folks. I was connected to the house in no time and was glad to hear my sister Alice's voice. At first she did not seem excited but when I told her that I was being shipped out her voice raised up. It seemed that bad news prevailed in our conversation for as I told her that I was leaving New Jersey, heading for some place near St. Louis, Missouri, she told me that one of my favorite uncles, Uncle Louis, my mother's brother, had passed away. She closed our conversation by saying something that I thought would never happen. She told me that Thomas Bauknight, my ex-brother-in-law, her former husband, was supposed to be stationed at Jefferson Barracks and since I was going close to St. Louis that could be my probable destination. I never realized how true her words were until almost a day later.

I had never been further west than Wilkes-Barre, Pennsylvania. The whole idea of going west was becoming more and more interesting to me. On the way to Philadelphia, I saw few towns and relatively few houses; practically all appeared to be farm homes. There was plenty of empty land for someone to profit by sooner or later. It was not long before we entered the city of the row houses and compact buildings, the city of Brotherly Love. Just before we entered the station, I saw for the first time in my life a sight that frankly surprised me. I saw women working with picks and shovels raising and digging up railroad ties in the hot sun high on the railroad trestle. I was the type of person that didn't even like women working in factories, much less high atop a railroad trestle. This sight and its relation to the significance of the war began at that moment to play on my mind.

We soon pulled out of Philadelphia and headed westward, going up among the mountains and into a beautiful part of Pennsylvania. Being late spring, everything was bright with blooms and the touch of early summer. The trees were green and full, the grass sprung high, and mother nature seemed to be having the time of her life way up high in the hills, seemingly far from the devastating hand of man. I never knew before that there was such an abundance of good land to be seen all in one place. Every once in a while evidence of man's presence would show its worn out face in the form of some isolated home or some small desecrated village.

By that evening we had reached Allentown, Pennsylvania, where the weathered buildings of the small towns seemed to reflect the hardships of living. To me the whole area had a cold and solemn appearance carrying the battle scars of decay and gray black coal dust. It's funny how things that look low and rotten can, under the surface, be a citadel of historical, economic, and political significance.

During the stop in Allentown, we talked with an elderly looking porter who claimed he didn't need a watch for he knew by his long experience when and where the different trains would be arriving at the station. He audaciously boasted about the fact that he knew all the engineers and firemen on all the big time trains like the Commodore, the old Chicago Flyer, the St. Louis Blues, the Pennsylvanian, the B&O Express, and the best of them all the Twentieth Century Limited. He was an interesting fellow because he seemed so engulfed in his world of steam and steel and the sound of the diesel engine or the shrieking whistle of one of the fast eastern trains would send chills of contented excitement up and down his spine.

Our troop train continued west going higher into the mountainous part of Pennsylvania. Every once in a while we would see the remains of another old mining town. Some of those places still seemingly alive were made up of old shacks, gray-black machinery, and rusted coal cars. Occasionally, we saw wisps of smoke rising from one of the small buildings and a soot-covered worker making his way home. It all lent itself to an atmosphere of deadness and relative inactivity. Most of the work of the coal mining industry is not evidenced from the surface. By looking at that land, one would never realize that within the area hidden beneath the surface are broad veins of coal, an energy resource too valuable to estimate its worth.

The train began to settle down to rather smooth riding and soon the beautiful Allegheny River, wide, spacious, and powerful came into view. It must have been raining torrents for some time prior to our arrival for the river was swollen and the water, swerving and twisting downward, seeming bursting with anger as it carried all the loose obstacles that lay in its path. This sight made me think of the strength and meaningful significance of nature. How quiet and serene it could be at times, then at another period of the year it could become a raging terror! This fact seemed to be proof that man shall never win his battle over nature. Man is intelligent, through acquired characteristics, nature is intelligent through its own God-given power and this power is eternal. Now in the war with the Axis nations, man had diverted his attention from nature and its resources to mankind itself, seemingly hell bent on self-destruction.

On we sped, still moving west, seeing an occasional village or mining town. As we moved along I gained increasing respect for railroads. Where in the world would we be without them? Who would transport most of the foodstuff for our country, in such a relatively short time? Who would transport across country much of the manufactured goods, industrial materials, and all the various needs of industry, if it were not for the railroads? As I thought about this, I thought back to my study of the railroads and recalled parts of its history. I remembered the fight moving westward over this country, the battles with nature and the various construction worries. Further west there was the worry of Indian attacks too. In railroad building, I saw a people spirited beyond belief, overcoming all obstacles to achieve their goal. Then, after the railroads were completed and the owners realized their importance and the monopoly powers they enjoyed, the railroad titans begin showing favoritism toward certain industries and over charging others. This soon led to the crooked policy of high rates for short distances and vise-versa. Such a policy was begun because the far-western companies were paying these titans good sums of money to get their foodstuff and materials to the industrial east before the producers of the mid-west could do so. The railroads in their day not only got into competition with all other forms of travel, but were the indirect cause of the formation of the Granges and other bodies of producers who discovered that more could be achieved by uniting their power.

Lights began to dot the hillsides as night drew over us like a silent cover. It appeared that everyone out in this part of the country was turning in. After all, it was nighttime and there was complete darkness. Street lights? No. The people in the homes we passed in this area did not have the modern conveniences of the small towns and cities. I would imagine that they lived peacefully and quiet knowing and being a friend of others who lived near them, growing their food on the sloping hillside and living by their gracious faith in God. Into the night the train sped. When we were ordered to bed, I remained awake for a long time in the compartment I shared with three other soldiers and wondered, thought, and hoped. That night I sent a prayer up to the heavens and asked for guidance and happiness in the future. I fell into a slow but drowsy sleep and early the next morning we were awakened by the porter when he opened the door and said: "Okay soldiers, the Sergeant said get up and wash for chow, because you have to get off at St. Louis in an hour!"

Well, the porter told us we would be getting off at St. Louis, Missouri, and he was right. Buses were waiting at the station for us. As we got on the bus, the word worked its way back through the bus that we were heading for Jefferson Barracks, Missouri, a base located in a suburban area just outside of the city limits of St. Louis. When we arrived at Jefferson Barracks, I thought we were coming into something that looked like a concentration camp. The reception area looked desolate. Outside of the steel fencing was that silent moving historic, mighty Mississippi River. I wondered had it ever overrun its banks in this part of the state. Further up into the base, we noticed more life, a few WACs, a squadron of soldiers marching in full precision, and a jeep speeding along the road. As we marched further into the camp, I felt better about the location. It began to look like a college campus, large green tracts of grass, beautiful old red buildings, all of which were trimmed by green ivy. Everything was uniform in nature.

Finally, after marching for what seemed like hours, we reached the "colored area" of the post. The first words I heard were from a soldier who stuck his head out of a barracks window yelling, "Hey, you 'cruits, you won't like it here." That phrase seemed to be a favorite of many soldiers for everywhere we went, we heard, "You won't like it here." That night when I retired those words kept ringing in my ears.

During the next few days, I did nothing but write letters, eat, and sleep. This two-week period of relative inactivity was called the Orientation Period. It is during this time that the soldier gets better acquainted with his fellow mates and the surrounding environment. We saw plenty of movies on military matters, sort of an indoctrination dealing with subjects like the Articles of War, drilling, military courtesy, and sexual morality. The only marching we did was to and from various parts of the post. The one thing I noticed and liked immediately was the singing of some of the marching men. One would never realize how much benefit there is from this singing while marching. It helps the soldier forget his worries, helps him forget the miles of marching, and helps to keep him in the best of spirits. I thought I had heard some good singing before I came into the army until I heard the black soldiers from Mississippi and Alabama. Those soldiers from the Deep South could really sing. They were not just singing for the hell of it, it seemed to come from the very depth of their souls.

Hand me down, (hand me down), hand me down,
(hand me down);
Hand me down my silver trumpet, Gabriel
Hand it down, throw it down, any way you get it
down
Hand me down my silver trumpet, Lord.

With their bodies, arms and legs moving in sync with the music as they marched up the road, they sang it with deep, personal feeling. The sound of their voices in unison seemed to echo off the clouds. It was like a glorious innovation in music, something I had never heard the likes of before.

As soon as I hit Jefferson Barracks, I thought about my sister Alice and her last words on the telephone. "That's where Thomas is suppose to be." I was very anxious to see him, for we had celebrated his leaving for the service back in April. When I was settled at the Barracks and understood about the training grounds, I went to the Service Club to inquire about the whereabouts of Private Thomas H. Bauknight. As soon as the Corporal said 1166th Training Group, I dashed out of the door and over to the 1166th quarters. In no time I found the barracks he was in. I went in the back door and went slowly down the aisle. Lo and behold, there on the first bed was my former brother-in-law, Thomas Bauknight. He did not see me at first and when he did I was standing by his side. I simply smiled, held out my hand and said, "Hi Buddie!" He looked at me as if he had seen a ghost. He was shocked! He appeared not to believe it at first, and he kept on looking at me strangely murmuring, "No. No. No. It can't be. No. Jimmy here. No, I can't believe it." In little time he came to his senses and was up on his feet, hugging me like a long lost brother. I am sure no other two people at that time were happier seeing each other. We sat and talked for the longest time. As we chatted amiably, the night guard came walking around, yelling, "Hey in there, put those lights out!" I said so long to Thomas and headed back to my quarters. Funny thing though, we both said we would look forward to seeing each other again while at the Barracks, but somehow, we never did.

Thomas and I did see each other at the old homestead, 47 Johnson Avenue, Cranford, during one of the furloughs. I did not see him again until I saw him after the war in Wilkes Barre, Pennsylvania. Tom and his best friend opened up a jewelry store in downtown Wilkes Barre where they featured beautiful jewelry and interesting clocks framed in bright shiny sculptured anthracite coal. I was very impressed with the store that was located down town amidst other fine shops. After opening his store, he married again to a lovely lady and spent his vacation time traveling to various resorts. I always liked Thomas and never felt that he was the cause of the divorce from my sister Alice.

Most of the days of my early training I spent learning to drill. When we began we resembled some kind of ragged misinterpretation for humankind, but, within a few weeks, precision started to set in and we were soon the pride of the training base. To become a bit technical, our training consisted of a lot of marching drills, a lot of calisthenics, occasional movies, and military lectures. The later stages of training included working with gas masks, learning about camouflage, the use of the pistol, the carbine, a 30 mm rifle, and the Thompson sub-machine gun. Most of the men, when they left Jefferson Barracks, were attached to engineering units or to various working units of the Army Air Force.

The layout at Jefferson Barracks was a very good one. The camp settled nicely on a huge plot along the shore of the Mississippi. There was plenty of foliage and rolling hillsides. The living quarters were roomy and rather comfortable for a military training situation. The barracks were lined along the road. There were four main offshoots of buildings and in the center there was a large mess hall, a chapel, a cinema, a service club, and a large drilling green. Down the main road were the buildings that housed the unit personnel offices, as well as, the 95th Wing Headquarters. Everything was like a small town where different soldier groups went through their stages of special training.

After 20 days of training, I began to get restless and just wanted to go home. I had a chance to ask for a permanent party assignment, but I did not seek it, for I did not want anything to hamper my leaving Jefferson Barracks. I never realized that I would soon have no say in what my destiny would be. About three days later, I was out in the field at a firing range getting ready to fire the rifle at moving wooden targets when I was told to report to the 95th Wing Headquarters. I arrived there in a cold sweat wondering what was up. After talking with a Captain Pritchard, I found that I had been selected with a group of soldiers who had college training to join the 95th Wing Headquarters Personnel

Unit and become a Permanent Party member. My training days were over, I was now assigned to a personnel records section that processed the records of soldiers coming on the post as well as those leaving for various assignment. I was stuck with being at Jefferson Barracks longer than I had imagined.

Jim Avery, corporal in the U.S. Army

June 17, 1943, I was assigned to the Personnel Office of the Headquarters 95th Training Wing Army Air Force Central Technical Training Command, Basic Training Center, Number 1, Jefferson Barracks, Missouri. Even before I began the work, I felt I was going to enjoy doing it. The group to which I was assigned appeared to be a special one. Of all the men in this colored section of the post, the Detachment Permanent Party men were the ones who got the most privileges and the most advantages. The fellows grew to feel they were better than the other soldiers. Several of the men had their college degrees. One was about to get his law degree. Many were Non-commissioned Officers (Noncoms) with more time in the service. Several in the Detachment were OCS washouts.

I found the fellows to be very congenial and quite informal even on my first day. They quickly began to give me the lowdown on officers and on those soldiers who were considered tattletales. It did not take me long to find out which fellows to be chummy with and which ones to neglect. I took the opinions of the so-called good guys with a grain of salt and allowed emerging situations to form the real feelings I had about people, conditions, and things.

I was put to work almost immediately in the Locator Department, which was rather small. A Sgt. Wilbur Benson

Strayhorn was in charge of this unit. He hailed from Chicago. He told me about his mother, and I could see that he loved her very much. He said she knew his every desire, his every dislike, and she cried a thousand tears every time he had a problem. He grew up with glowing respect for her and her ideals. He was gifted with her common sense quality and her ideas about the various aspects of life.

During this time my father and I wrote quite often to each other. The letters from my dad were like manna from heaven, filling a void of loneliness that weighed so heavily upon me since leaving home for military service four months before. My father's words were not complex or hard to comprehend, their content conveyed the dignity of his love and pride that seemed to energize my spirit. Each time in my response, I told him of my deep and abiding love for him, but it seemed I could never quite say it the way he would say it to me in the letters I still have in my memorabilia. How difficult it must have been for my dad to have four sons in the army during World War II and how much he must have worried and prayed for us. Even though he missed us terribly, he told us to do the very best job we could in our respective roles. In a letter he wrote dated July 29, 1943, he said; "Dear Son James, I hope you will not feel bad of me for using a pencil to write this letter. I am enjoying good health at this time and hope when this (letter) comes to hand it may find you the same, happy, and well. From the letters you write it shows that you are doing fine work. So my advice is to keep up the good work, go as far as you can and do the best that you can. I have great faith in you for both your mother and I did the best we could to make it possible for you to get ahead in the world." In another letter in November of 1943 he said, "Now James, I am truly proud of every child I have and will do my best for them. So trust in God and he will bring you out all right. Every one is fine here and joins me in great love to the great boy which you are, this from Dad." One cannot imagine how touched I was when in one letter to me he wrote: "I am hoping and looking forward to seeing you that I may greet my baby boy, the hundred and eighty pounds face to face." How I treasure those letters he wrote, even as they become more yellowed and frayed and precious.

I went into the personnel group with several fellows I knew from the 1167 Training Wing. One of them was a good friend, Wilfred Biagas. Biagas was from New Orleans, Louisiana. He was a very resourceful and intelligent man with an IQ of 150! In his past life he must have been very happy, carefree, and spoiled by devoted parents. "Big," as I soon nicknamed him, had a very retentive mind. No one person knew as much about sports and about sports figures as he. That guy could tell you who had run the ball on every Rose Bowl touchdown for the last ten years. He had the facility of naming more college football players than I could read about in three sports books. He knew so much, including many of the records and who made them. Biagas and I became great buddies and spent a lot of off duty time together.

Now a permanent party man, I found myself free to go to town any night I saw fit. As a trainee, you could not go when you felt like it. St. Louis was like a lot of cities where blacks could be found living essentially in one area. In this city they lived mostly in the northeast, an area extending over to the northwest part of the city. The wealth of the people seemed to increase as you went further west and so did the fine homes, most of them made of brick, and fine cars. In the east side, the people, while not living in the depth of poverty, were less fortunate. In my own observations, I found that the blacks who were moving further westward were living in homes formerly occupied by whites. The process was slow, but as one or two blacks moved into the area, whites moved further out. The ghetto was getting larger in the sense that as blacks began to move out into the fringes of the ghetto into better homes, the seediness of the core area was spreading too. I was seeing, in a very vivid way, the social-economic condition that would be the basic reason for continuing racial problems for years to come.

Speaking of people in the city of St. Louis, the first really nice people I met was through the efforts of a friend of mine from my old training group the 1167th Wing, Eddie Davis. He, too, was from New Orleans, medium build, good looking and a high-powered ladies' man. He met a young lady named Ermine Bush at the Service Club one night and inside of two weeks there was a thriving romance. One day I asked him about Ermine's sister. You know, the general routine questions about her looks, her personality, and boyfriends. I asked him so much about her that he saw to it that I was invited to the Bush residence for dinner one Sunday afternoon. That Sunday came and went without a dinner because, unfortunately, I could not make it. I felt very bad about it, more so when he told me they had waited for me and had an opera ticket for me that evening. I knew then I had an apology to make and, the following week, I arrived at the Bush residence with my hat in hand, apologized and sat down to a very interesting evening. I met Ermine's sister Margaret Bush that night and when I left, I made it my business to return at a later date. I had many dates after that first night with Margaret, who proved to be a very interesting and attractive young lady. In professional life she was a lawyer, a graduate of Talladega College and Lincoln University (Missouri), School of Law. She was in a practice with another lawyer in the city. During her college days she had studied abroad in India, France, and England. There was no doubt she was a brilliant person. We went many places, bowling, operas, baseball games, etc. When I went to visit and we stayed at home, we did not make out like many fortunate guys would do; instead she liked to play word games. She was great at it, and I must admit I was fairly good but not her equal. We had good times together, but there was something missing, something that seemed to keep things from going any further than just being a routine platonic relationship and an extremely respectful friendship. We began to drift apart as I met others with whom, for some unspecified reason, I felt more at ease. Margaret Bush and I remained friends over the years. She married a fellow named Wilson and later became Chairman of the Board of the NAACP. I last talked with her when I was in St. Louis in 1973 for an Omega Psi Phi Fraternity national meeting, known as the "Conclave." Interestingly, Margaret's sister Ermine married a dentist in Rochester, New York, a man named Tommy Irons, who was a fraternity brother of mine.

I met other ladies at the USO, dated some but never got serious about any of them. At one time while I was at Jefferson Barracks, Mary Ella came out from New Jersey for a visit. We had a great time seeing the city. There were two beautiful ladies from New Orleans that I met and dated, Elise Cain and Velma Burke. I remained very close friends with them for many years after the war. In some ways, New Orleans was a favorite city for me to get to know people I enjoyed being with. There were several soldiers I met and grew friendly with from that city, guys like: Eddie Davis, Joe Arnaud, Guy Daste, Joe McKelpin, and Asa Akins. All these guys were wonderful friends with wonderful families that I got to know when I visited the Crescent City.

Jefferson Barracks was my home for about a year. Each day, after duty hours, when I stayed on the post, I spent my time loafing, reading, or running the obstacle course with Harrison Dillard, a fellow soldier who was a famous Olympic hurdler. Harrison and I had a great deal of fun running the course and it helped us stay in wonderful shape. Harrison Dillard went back to Cleveland, Ohio, and became world famous for his hurdling ability after the war. Unfortunately, while I read great things about him, we never had the opportunity to visit and share experiences.

I enjoyed the city, particularly the sports venues and wonderful Forest Park in the city of St. Louis, where I could sit on the grass and see and listen to musical programs like Desert Song with the movie actor Nelson Eddy. One must remember that musical shows of those times were much different than what we would see today. If I were to go to Forest Park today, I would probably see performers like "Chicago" or the lovely Anita Baker.

In May, I learned we were going to be shipped out with soldiers going to different bases around the country. We talked about places like Scott Field in Illinois and the base in Madison, Wisconsin, as two favorite locations. For me, it was not to be, for one night I found myself getting on a military train that was going south, destination unknown.

The train ride was a very unpleasant experience. We slept in bunk-like beds put up in rows in cars that looked more like those that transport cattle. There were other cars where tables were set up for military mess. There were no lounge cars where we could just sit and look out the windows. We had to see what was passing outside by looking out the windows from our bunk beds. I remember with some trepidation seeing a number of white supremacy billboard signs as we went deeper and deeper into the South. The further south we went, the hotter it got. The trees began to change to palm trees and orange groves. We knew then we were in Florida and going south in that state. Finally, when the train stopped, we were in Boca Raton, Florida, destined for Boca Raton Army Air Base.

Boca Raton was an area that essentially was and still is a resort area. In fact, the Boca Raton Club was located there and still is one of the wealthiest high society clubs in the country. Palm Beach County, an area of considerable wealth, was not too far north. Army buses took us from the train station to the base where we were taken to Section F where the black soldiers were housed. Most of the black soldiers assigned to that section did the muscle work on the base. Those of us who were Permanent Party members were an exception since our job was to process the records of soldiers coming in and being shipped out. Most of us in the Records group were housed in the same barracks building. The unfortunate part of this was that we were under a sergeant from the backwoods of North Carolina. Sergeant Montgomery was his name. He hated those of us with college training and sought in many ways to demean us with latrine work and floor scrubbing. He was the meanest fellow I ever met in the service or anywhere else and I have often wondered whatever happened to him when the war was over.

I became a good friend of a fellow soldier named Alvin Tinnin. Al was from White Plains, New York, and we spent a lot of free time together. Al had attended Talladega College prior to the war but did not complete his degree. We went on our furlough together on the same train north. I recall meeting him in New York City to go up to his home in White Plains. We went up to Harlem to have a few drinks before getting on the train at 125th Street. We ended up at Small's Paradise drinking a mixture of rum and other liquors that had a special name I cannot recall. If I were to guess, I would say we were drinking Boilermakers or Blockbusters. We got on the train at 125th Street somehow and in some kind of a stupor fell asleep. The next thing we knew, the conductor was waking up both of us in New

Haven, Connecticut, asking if we had gone past our station. Somehow, we got back to White Plains, I don't remember how. I vowed never to try that combination of liquors again! My visit to his home was a real pleasure and his Mom and Dad were extremely nice people. At the end of our furloughs, we met on the train for our trip back to the base in Florida. When we were in Georgia and just about to go into Florida, Al Tinnin had just about enough of the segregated car and the shades that had to be pulled down on the windows where we ate our food once we got into the South. We were not allowed to see outside of the colored dining car and obviously anyone outside could not see us, as if seeing us would make whites throw up or flee in horror. Al was steadily complaining about being a soldier and having to suffer such indignities. Fully aware of the stinking situation, I tried to get him to cool down. Not Al, he got up and went into the next car to complain. He did not come back for the longest time. After eating and going back to the car where we had seats, I noted the train had reached one of the stations in Florida. I looked out the window and behold, there was Al in handcuffs between two white MPs being taken from the train and he was still arguing his point as they took him away. Several days later back at the base, I saw him and he told me that he had had some words with the MPs about the segregated conditions with which black soldiers had to deal and his words got him into trouble.

Joe Murphy from St. Louis was another fellow on the base whom Al and I got to know very well. Later on we used to sit around the piano and harmonize with Joe, Sergeant William Whiteside, who hailed from Minneapolis, Minnesota, and Maurice Morris from a town in Texas. Joe Murphy, who was a trained musician, was the only one who could read music, and somehow he got us started on singing songs in close harmony. Since we could not read music, we had to learn via a rote system. Under Joe's guidance we became quite good and were asked by Personnel to be a part of the entertainment group on the post. We called ourselves "The Dreamers" and had a theme song with words that went something like this:

The Dreamers, the Dreamers
You wonder who we are
Why ask us, what for,
We'll always be the Dreamers
'Til we dream no more.

Spotlight Time, as the entertainment was called by Personnel, was held at the Open Air Theater in the Central Area before thousands of soldiers. As the post newspaper, *The Transmitter,* dated October 4, 1944 stated:

> Jolting jive keynoted by the work of "The Dreamers" and Private Bennie Payne, all of Section F, made for a successful revue last Friday night. After a soldier did a distinctly different tap routine, followed by a soloist from Section L, The Dreamers and Bennie Payne took over. Payne was a wonderful jazz pianist formerly featured with Cab Calloway. The quintet did "San Fernando Valley," "Some day I'll Meet You Again," and "Getting Sentimental Over You." Next "The Dreamers" teamed up with Bennie Payne as he sang, "Ole Man Moses," "Straighten Up and Fly Right" and "Ain't Misbehavin."

Corporal Charlie Banks was another entertainer who joined the Spotlight Time entertainment group. Banks was a fine tap dancer who previously had understudied the great Bill Robinson in the Hot Mikado. The post newspaper said:

> The Dreamers with Bennie Payne and his ensemble and Charlie Banks and some dancers became a great hit on the post and each Wednesday evening thousands of soldiers gathered in the Open Air Theater for the entertainment.

Later in the year, Tony Martin, the singing movie star, was assigned to our base. In no time Tony joined Spotlight Time as the featured performer. Tony was a warm and engaging fellow who was not condescending in any way in his relationship with us. It was wonderful having him as part of the entertaining team. While we never did it, it was Tony who told us that we were good and that we should stay together as a singing group and build up a large inventory of music and then try to go big time. There was a guy there who had been with a New York City radio station, WOV, who said the same thing to us.

The Personnel Group that was responsible for arranging the entertainment for the soldiers on the base, also made arrangements for our musical aggregation to perform on weekends for soldiers stationed in various places in South Florida. We, The Dreamers, along with Tony Martin, Bennie Payne and his ensemble, Charlie Banks, and other dancers had a ball doing these weekend gigs.

We never did go off into the hinterlands of America and build up a repertoire as Tony Martin and the guy from the New York City radio station WOV suggested. The Dreamers were disbanded when Joe Murphy's term of service ended and his wife did not want him to continue the activity. Al Tinnin was the only one who continued in music. He went to New York and was on Broadway in the musical "Call Me Mister" starring Betty Garrett and Bert Parks. After the war, Al and I remained good friends and stayed in touch with each other. Al later attended Carlton College in Northfield, Minnesota, and majored in French. He spent time in France and returned to teach at Yale University before going out to be a part of the Language Department at the College of Redlands in Redlands, California. After his retirement from Redlands, he and I had an opportunity to visit at my home in Scotch Plains, New Jersey, and renew fond memories. I never saw or heard from Joe Murphy, William Whiteside, or Maurice Moore once I left Boca Raton Army Air Base.

The Dreamers musical group was not the only thing that I did in my off time at Boca Raton. I loved sports and participated on the Section F touch football team and the basketball team. I was chosen to be on the Post All-Star team based on my play during the season. On Thanksgiving Day in November 1944, the All-Star Team played the undefeated Section P team. I threw two touchdown passes, and we defeated them 20-18. Later the post newspaper, *The TRANSMITTER*, named me the All-Around Athlete of Boca Raton Army Air Base. The post paper sent this information to the *Cranford Chronicle* that published the following article.

Post Newspaper Article

PFC Avery Cited for Athletic Record

Private James Avery, son of John Avery of 47 Johnson Avenue and the late Mrs. Avery has been voted the most outstanding athlete at Boca Raton AAF, Florida, according to a recent article on the sports page of the field newspaper. He is star of the squadron field basketball team. The local athlete was voted all-state quarterback of the 1940 season when he was star of the Cranford High School team and he completed more passes than any other player in the state that year.

He received all-state honorable mention in basketball. Avery was president of the Student Council of the local high school. He attended Columbia University before enlisting in the army in 1942. While in college he played on the freshman football and basketball teams and ran the hurdles on the track team. He was on the Columbia College varsity football team in his Sophomore year as a reserved fullback until he was injured in a scrimmage before the Cornell game.

Private Avery entered the armed forces on May 12, 1943, and is with the Army Air Corps. He has three brothers in the armed forces: Sgt. Louis Avery with the Army in France; Cpl. Friend Avery, formerly with the army in New Guinea and now at an unknown location in the Pacific; and John Avery in the U.S. Naval Shore Patrol at Newport, Rhode Island.

Several months after I arrived at Boca Raton AAF in 1943, I met Sue Butler from West Palm Beach, Florida. She was a beautiful young lady with a great personality. We fell in love, at least I thought we did, and in April 1945 were married in a quiet ceremony at her home. Maurice Moore, who was one of the Dreamers, was my best man. I think it was Sue's beauty that blew my mind. At the time, I was too blind to see that physical attraction alone was not strong enough to make the marriage last. We really did not have much in common. I loved to play sports. I loved to watch sports. She was not interested in sports nor was she particularly interested in major issues of the day. The physical attraction was so strong that it blinded me to everything else. Sue had a lovely personality that endeared her to everyone she met. Her mom was one of the sweetest ladies I have ever known. Her sister Dorothy was a fun person too. The unstable circumstances of the army, the war and all, did not help. In the summer of 1945, I came back to the base after a furlough to find that I was being shipped out to McDill Field outside of Tampa, Florida. I left Sue with her mother in West Palm Beach not knowing what my ultimate destiny was going to be. Once I got there and knew I was not going to be shipped out soon, I looked into an apartment for Sue and me in the city of Tampa, but nothing satisfactory ever surfaced. As a result I just stayed on the post and Sue stayed in West Palm Beach. I would see her at every opportunity I had to get back to West Palm Beach.

At McDill Field, I was placed in the Permanent Party unit assigned to the Records Section. I did not waste any time getting involved with sports. I joined the softball team of the Engineering Aviation Unit Training Command. We became the softball champions of McDill Field that year. I played on that team with fellows who would later become my teammates on the post football and basketball teams.

I had heard about the post football team and looked forward to the announcement for the start of football practice for the McDill Field Bulldozers. Naturally, I signed up for the team as soon as I could do so. After long, nightly practices in the field behind the EAUTC Headquarters with an outstanding group of guys, many of whom had played for various black colleges in the nation, I was finally selected as a starting halfback. Our head coach was Sgt. "Pinky" Clark, a former Assistant Coach at Morgan State College in Baltimore, Maryland. Our quarterback, who was actually like a blocking back in the system Coach Clark used, was Paul Hutchinson, who had played at both Morgan State and Arkansas State. Hulon Willis, a fantastic athlete, was our starting center and played his college ball at Virginia State. Lester Eaton, a tackle, had played at Bishop College. A starting guard, George Russell, had played at Kentucky State College. Hank Johnson was a tackle who hailed from Ithaca College. Leroy Hambric was a halfback who had played at Clark College. Leroy Moore was an end who had played for Langston University. George Barrett, a running back, had played at Lane College. Those were just the guys with college training. We had some fine ball players who only had experience at the high school level.

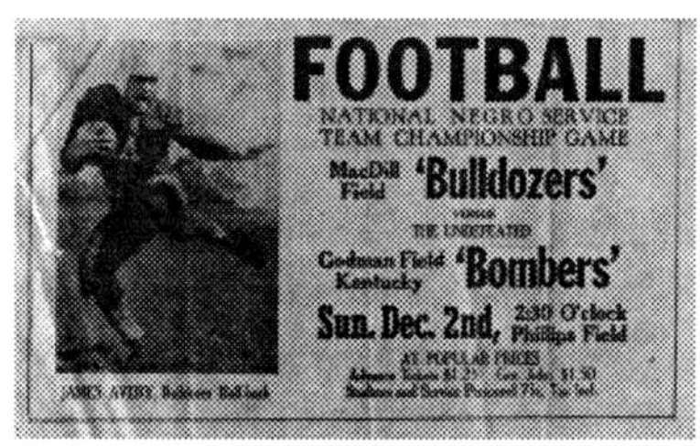

Newspaper Announcement of the McDill Field Bulldozers championship game

We played eight games that year losing one and that came by a single touchdown to a team we had beaten earlier in the season 19–0. Our toughest contest was our game with the Tuskegee AAF Warhawks, a team composed mostly of commissioned officers who were pilots. We, of course, were noncoms and privates. I do not think I have ever been in a game more like a small war, officers against mostly privates, each trying to beat the other. Somehow, through all the bloody grime of the Vulcan Bowl in Birmingham, Alabama, we came out with a hard fought 6 to 0 victory. Both teams left that field with great respect for each other. Since we had beaten the Tuskegee AAB Warhawks, the Fort Benning, Georgia, Tigers, Jacksonville Naval Station, Robbins Field in Florida, and Randolph Field from Texas. We had to play the Godman Field Bombers from Kentucky to determine who would become the National Negro Service Champions. The Base Commander of Godman Field was the very famous black General, Benjamin O. Davis, Jr. I had looked forward to meeting this famous general, but he did not come to Tampa with his base's team. We played Godman

Field before a sell out crowd at Phillips Field in Tampa, Florida. I can recall that at half time, the score was 13–7 in our favor. Coach Pinky Clark came into our dressing room and said some words that I have never forgotten. I have always believed that those words encouraged us to go out of that locker room like a pack of wild dogs ready to devour whatever came in sight. We played our asses off that second half and won that tough game 24 to 14 and the championship. Whenever memory recalls the great playing of the McDill Field Bulldozers, Coach Clark's words always echo softly in the background.

Do not pray for easy lives
Pray to be stronger men.
Do not pray for tasks equal to your powers,
Pray for power equal to your tasks.
Then the doing of your tasks will be no miracle.
For you shall be the miracle…
And every day you will glory in the power
That has come to you
Through the grace of God!

After that game we received all sorts of accolades from the citizens of Tampa, Florida, from fellow soldiers, the press, and our superior officers. I recall the letter each member of the football team received from the Base Commanding Officer, R. J. Burt. The letter I received stated:

> To: PFC James Avery:
>
> The Commanding Officer takes great pleasure in forwarding to you the above commendation. You are to be congratulated on the part you played in making this team an outstanding example of the spirit of the American soldier.

After the football season ended, I went over to the gym and signed up for the McDill Field basketball team. When the regular season started, there were 14 of us who made the team. It was a great bunch of guys and included some well-known players too. "Goose" Tatum was our center. Goose had played for the world famous Harlem Globetrotters. Tom Sealy had starred for the famous Renaissance team in New York. (After the war ended, Goose Tatum went back to play with the Globetrotters.) Sergeant McGirt was our coach and had been deeply involved in the sport in the New York City area. We traveled all over the east and as far as Texas to play other army posts. It was a lot of fun and fortunately, we won most of our games. There was no real league as we had in football, so there was no such thing as a basketball champion. If there had been, we would have been right up there at the top of the league.

VII

Back to Columbia

Early in 1945, knowing I was going to go back to Columbia after the war, I wrote to the Columbia College coach, Lou Little. Lou Little was one of the best known and greatest football coaches in America. In 1935, the Columbia Lions had a great team, and he took them to the Rose Bowl and defeated Stanford, 6 to 0, in a thriller. Sid Luckman was the All-American quarterback on that team. In later years, Sid, who was one of the warmest guys it was my pleasure ever to know, was a great pro quarterback for the Chicago Bears. Lou Little and I corresponded every so often in 1945 and in early 1946. I still have four of the very personal letters he wrote to me, and I treasure them. I know he wanted me back as a player, but as he would always put it, as a student first.

On February 14, 1946, via Special Orders # 25, I was transferred in grade along with 21 other soldiers to ASF Separation Center, Camp Blanding, Florida, for discharge from the United States Army. Following my discharge, I spent some time at my wife Sue's home in West Palm Beach, Florida. Sometime in the late spring, I took Sue with me back to my home in Cranford, New Jersey. We lived at 47 Johnson Avenue for a while, but because of the lack of room, we moved up the street to an apartment in the home of an older, well-liked couple named Mr. and Mrs. Edward Oliver.

In the fall of 1946, I went back to Columbia to continue my education. I went to visit Lou Little to discuss playing football for him at Columbia. I explained that I was now married and needed some kind of job to earn extra money while I was attending college. There were about 15 former players who claimed the need of some type of added income at that time for various reasons. Lou pointed out that he could not offer us any special scholarships or special jobs. If we were going to play, then we would have to decide to do so on our own as student athletes. I was one of the former players who decided to forego football and focus time on classes and other student activities. I did just that and had good grades and was chosen to be a member of one of the two special student leadership groups on the campus. One of the groups was named NACHEMS and the other society to which I was elected was called the SACHEMS. Both organizations still exist but I no longer attend their yearly functions.

Graduation yearbook photograph, Columbia College, 1948

I got my bachelor of arts degree in June of 1948 and continued with graduate studies to get my master of arts degree in education with a minor in history in December of 1949. I felt extremely proud to have two degrees from such a great, world-renowned university as Columbia. I think I was most proud when I got my bachelor's degree in May of 1948, and my father was there with me. Sue did not come, and I really cannot recall the reason. I felt that my mother was with me in spirit. After the graduation ceremonies, my father and I walked around the campus so I could show him many of the imposing buildings where I had taken courses. I could feel his pride, but I think I was proudest just to have him with me that day. Here he was a son of a slave, a slave who was owned by his white plantation owner father, essentially unlettered himself, walking around the grounds of one of the world's greatest universities with his son who had just graduated with a bachelor's degree.

During my years as a student at Columbia, I had great professors, such as Dr. Lawrence Chamberlain, who taught government with all of its political drama. There was also Dr. Krout of the Graduate Faculties, who taught American history in intimate detail without notes or a book. Dr. Erling M. Hunt of Columbia University's Teachers College was another outstanding teacher scholar who taught me the great value of systematic reasoning. My sociology, French, and psychology professors were all excellent too. It is the outstanding teaching and mind-molding that makes Columbia one of the greatest educational institutions. I could not recite all the things that those professors taught me or tell you details about the specifics of the Greek works I read by the great historian, Herodotus, or the poet, Euripides, to name a few. I just enjoyed them immensely. Yet I gained insight from each experience that helped me become a more intelligent individual who has a better sense of artistic values, of analytical thinking, and of reasoning before attending Columbia University. While I was not on the dean's honor roll, I did get an A+ in a sociology course. Whatever I learned, it just engulfed me. I don't recall that my learning came in any pattern or shape.

Columbia, like many universities, was a place where students held divergent views about life, including those who were godless and those who lacked a positive sense of self. I can recall the presence of young radicals at Columbia who invaded every liberal, interracial group on the campus, seeking to spread the doctrines they believed. There were some who fell victims to the radical philosophies. I have always believed that one should have an open mind and be receptive to new ideas based upon good common sense. The good student tries to understand why people think, act and feel as they do. Recognizing that the mind must be intelligent enough to possess that filtering agent that, in weighing the ideas against standards of good and bad, against progress or regression, or the formation of opinions without facts, filters out what is inconsistent with the intelligent learning process. As some bright mind once said, we should be "firmly aware that there are ways to cope with the feelings that are wholesome for us and not harmful to others while maintaining a firm belief in something greater than ourselves." At Columbia, the successful student learns to think rationally and evaluate sensibly in determining vital decisions on life.

Friendships were another wonderful thing about going to college. Sometimes those friendships were singular in nature and rather exclusive. When I returned to complete my bachelor's degree at Columbia in the fall of 1946, I had a roommate named Harold L. Tapley, a bright young man from Peekskill, New York. From the very first day we met, we got along famously and had many wonderful experiences that we laugh about even today. Despite the various, changing movements of our lives, Harold and I remained in contact and have remained close friends through the years. "Tap," my nickname for him, graduated as an engineer. After five years in that field, he decided he wanted to be a doctor. He went to Howard University Medical School and ultimately became an anesthesiologist practicing in New York and later in California. Dr. Tapley did an additional residency in psychiatry and is practicing in California, where he has an outstanding reputation in his field. Not only that, he hits the damn golf ball farther than I can! He is an amazing guy whom I love as a friend and respect as a very intelligent human being. We see each other whenever the opportunity permits, and it is always the good ole days when we are together.

Jim Avery with his Columbia College roommate, Harold L. Tapley

While I was getting my master's degree, I had to spend a great deal of time at Columbia, particularly in the libraries. I often got home late and seldom had enough time for my wife Sue. In a way, it was not fair to her to live in Cranford without much to do or a job that she could get. I felt so guilty about that because I had not planned well at all, especially not like an intelligent person with a college education. The change in the environment for her was very traumatic. She was thrust among people who were loving and kind, but it still was not like home for her. She was the youngest daughter of three, and her mother and sisters doted on her. Not having much to do in Cranford, she spent a great deal of time with her brother in New York City. I sensed her unhappiness and knew that the only way she could be happy was to live in Florida near her siblings. I wanted her with me and begged her to just let me finish my education, and we could make plans together for the future. Her mother tried to convince her to stay too. I did not want our marriage to dissolve. I even talked to her about taking college courses that could give her a basis for a career in a field of her liking. She did not want to. The straw that broke the camel's back was the time I took away from her in pursuing my master's degree. I was devastated when Sue finally left me and went to live for a while with her brother in New York City. I did my best to get her to give me time and come back to Cranford while I finished my education. She said she just wasn't ready for the loneliness and the restricted situation that marriage to me brought about. We had no children and life in a small town like Cranford without an interest in something must have been extremely dull for her, more than I ever realized. Sue finally went back to her mother's home in West Palm Beach, Florida. I had an awful time getting my focus back on the courses I was taking at Columbia. I just had to get those degrees, I knew that I would not be any good to myself or anyone else if I did not continue in school and make the grades at Columbia. Regrettably, Sue and I decided to end our marriage. I asked a former army buddy, Pervil Eastman, who was a New York lawyer, to handle the divorce, and he took care of it in an effective and quiet manner in 1950.

Sue had an aunt living in Plainfield, New Jersey, and during a visit 30 years later she went to see my brother Friend, always a favorite of hers. I was living in Scotch Plains and Friend brought Sue to visit me. She was now a mother, living in Delray, Florida, a neighboring community to West Palm Beach. Before she left that day she said that our breakup was really her fault. I did not agree with her at all. I told her I felt it takes two to tango and that with my determined focus on getting an education, I was to blame far more than she.

VIII

Playing Sports, Teaching, Coaching

The immediate post war period was an interesting one. My best buddy Steve, and Curtis Durham and Thomas Woody, two other friends who lived in Cranford, were the fellows that I spent a lot of time with in the summer months right after the war. Three of us, Steve, Curtis, and I, took jobs in a furniture factory in neighboring Clark, New Jersey. Woody worked in a liquor store. After some training I became a competent paint sprayer of bed slats and headboards. It wasn't an easy job because I was spraying paint stain and had to use hand, arm, and foot movements on a spinning stand in concert with each other and not leave any stain blotches on the wood. Like anything else I tried to do, I kept at it until I got to the point where I never had furniture pieces rejected. A fellow named Schlacter owned the company, and he knew that I wanted to go back to Columbia for the fall semester. At the end of summer, he gave me what he called a scholarship of several hundred dollars to use for books and other needs. I never forgot his generosity. When I graduated with my master's degree, I went back to the factory to show it to him, but it was gone.

Tommy, Curtis, Woody, and I all liked music and talked about it a lot. Woody played a trumpet. Curt liked the drums. Steve and I could not play any instrument. I remember one time when we were talking about some music we all liked, a beautiful number called "Sunset" from Part 4 of the *Grand Canyon Suite* by Frede Grofe. Woody and Curtis asked me to put words to the music of "Sunset." I really don't think they felt they were going to get anything from me. I wrote the words and a preamble to help define the period of a sunset. It went like this:

Preamble:

We all know the changing beauty of the skies. We have looked in awe as a storm gathered its might in the heavens and have stood in a tranquil mood as a brilliant dawn or the inspiring radiance of a sunset cast its hypnotic glow. We can envisage in such a mood lovers dreaming of sky-born legends about silvery stars and undying love. During the day we have looked at the clouds, seeing them as if they were appearing on a vast blue stage. They look like dancers that melt, change and pirouette into many patterns and shapes. No greater beauty can be seen than a sunset's closing pageantry. It is truly the story of a symphony that never dies, a symphony that seems to carry a message of eternal faith.

To the music of "Sunset," I wrote:

At dawn the Painted Desert brings
Its amber colors to the sky.
Two lovers strangely dreaming,
Of legends mutely gleaming,
And stars of silver, the words familiar,
Of endless love as true as heaven's blue.
And through the day the clouds become,
Like ballet dancers in the sky.
Drawn by celestial singing,
They pirouette, then clinging,
Melt all their magic in your eyes.
Then evening brings the dying sun,
To tell the world that day is done.
The closing pageant of the sky, the sunset's gift to
eventide, God's end of day just gone by.
The symphony that never dies.
The symphony that never dies. Sunset. Sunset.
Prelude to love . . . .

The fellows could not believe that I could write that in such a short span of time. I can't explain it. I had always loved the song, and it somehow gave me a picture of a beautiful sunset. I think that at some time, perhaps, in later years, someone wrote words that were copyrighted. Mine never were, but the guys felt that I should have tried to copyright mine. They thought the words were fantastic. I still think the words sound great with the music, even better than those that were copyrighted.

Leisure hours that summer were filled with a variety of social activities, all clustered around a group of young black men, most of whom lived in Cranford. We formed a club called The Avengers. While we had our club parties and social gatherings, what we enjoyed most was the softball team. The Avengers played in the town league and against teams from a few neighboring towns. I played shortstop and covered a wide range on that side of the infield. My brother Friend was the second baseman, and he loved it when he and I made a great double play. Russell "Plunk" Douglas played third base. Plunk, as we called Russell, wore a chain device on his right arm to keep his shoulder from moving too far out and dislocating. Jobie Richard was our first baseman. There was no one tougher than Jobie, and no one who loved to fight more than he or who got into as much trouble as he. The spectators loved it when Jobie would do the splits while reaching for a ball thrown to him at first base. They loved to see Plunk Douglas grab a hot liner down the third base line, hold it as if to intimidate the runner, and then throw him out at first base. My buddy Tommy Stevenson and Jesse Muldrow were two of the outfielders. Steve, as I called Tommy, was a wonderful player who eventually played on a semi-pro level and even went to tournaments in the Midwest. We had great fun playing softball. James Laurel was one of our pitchers, and he was fairly good. The other pitcher was Clarence Kelsey who threw

The Cranford New Jersey Avengers Softball Team, 1960. Jim Avery was the team shortstop

a very slow pitch, almost a lob, to the plate. You can imagine how busy we were in the field whenever Clarence pitched. Somehow, we eventually won the town league title, beating a team of white fellows called "The Maroons," who were our friends in everyday life but our enemies on the playing field.

After getting my bachelor's and master's degrees at Columbia University, I looked for jobs in a lot of places. Blacks at the time, unless they were professionals like doctors or lawyers, were not hired for white-collar jobs. Black guys with college training and advanced degrees worked in the post office or on the railroads as Pullman porters. I did not want to end up like that. I went to Dr. H.R. Best, who was still the Superintendent of Cranford Schools and told him the situation and asked for a job as a teacher. In the fall of 1949, Dr. Best hired me as a teacher in the Social Studies Department. I may have been the first black to be hired in a suburban high school anywhere in New Jersey. I knew the job carried with it a big responsibility to show that I could do the work and do it well. I relished the challenge. It's hard to say exactly how or why we as black people automatically feel the burden of such "pilot" circumstances and consequences. However, no one ever has to tell a thoughtful and reasonably perceptive black man what he is up against or the path he must beat for others who follow behind him. It's largely intuitive, in some respect hereditary. Don't get me wrong, I didn't like being "the only one." I didn't see any reason or obligation to feel proud of being the first symbol of desegregation in what was supposed to be an enlightened community. But, besides "visibility," I had some other things going for me that other white teachers new to the system did not have. I had gone to that school. I had been president of the student council. I had been fortunate enough to be an all-state athlete, a member of the National Honor Society, and a winner of a Charles Hayden Memorial Scholarship to Columbia College. I had left a good record. I damn well could not come back and louse it up. I loved that school, and I loved the responsibility given to me. However, I was very much concerned about how the students would react to my presence and how the teachers and parents would respond. After all, I would be introducing a change from the usual, almost imposing upon things considered accepted standards long nourished, even if nourished for the wrong reasons. Later in life, my daughter said something knowing that I had faced a number of "firsts" in my life and had succeeded in what I was asked to do. She said that I "was a person who was comfortable in my own skin." Maybe that is why I did succeed. I was never intimidated by situations like that. Then again, fortunately, despite the fact that I was a black man, the fact that I had been a Cranford student and prominent athlete there made my acceptance easier.

When I started as a teacher in Cranford, I was not given a full load; in fact I worked in concert with Lydia Polglase, a fine person who was then chairperson of the Social Studies Department. She was an outstanding teacher, and I learned a great deal from her. I was also given the job of setting up the first driver education program the high school ever had. The Board of Education voted to incorporate such a course in the Cranford High School curriculum in the fall of 1949. The course was to be given in the spring to as many junior year students as possible, initially 130. The following year it was compulsory for all juniors. I developed a course of study that was presented to the Board of Education and approved. I had to do this using only classroom materials. The school decided not to purchase a dual-control automobile for the course, pointing out that the large number of students would permit a mere 15 minutes of actual driving time in a car for each one. Despite the absence of a car, the class was a successful one. Using various texts, charts, films, and other visual aids, we focused on the rules and regulations of the Department of Motor Vehicles, the tests that they would have to take, and on the aspects and attitudes of good safety-minded driving. I used a lot of films that showed what happened to those with bad driving habits. Some of the pictured accidents were horrible enough to scare the daylights of the students. All those who took the course passed their driving tests with flying colors! No one at the time knew that I did not own a car or that I could not drive a car where you had to shift gears. I kept those facts secret for the longest time.

Asst. Coach Avery (center) with members of the CHS 1954 football team, 2005 class reunion

Coaches Avery and Grayson, just out of the showers with three members of the championship team

Coach Jim Avery, with his Cranford High School's winning 1953 JV Team

In 1951, I began to have a full schedule of social studies classes and no longer taught driver education. I also began to coach the junior varsity football, to assist with the junior varsity basketball, and to help coach the track team. Naturally, I thoroughly enjoyed the coaching and had winning JV teams. I was not an easy coach. In my view one had to play tough and strong and see each task as something to accomplish at the highest level. To me, the practicing and the games themselves were like real life experiences. You faced your task with determination and guts and you did your best to come out on top. Giving up or taking the low road was not an option! My athletes had to understand that giving their best was the goal and that teamwork and respecting the contribution of the other players was of utmost importance. If that did not lead to winning, then they had to learn to live with it. Of course, playing the game correctly in a determined, blood and guts manner most often resulted in victory. The kids that I coached lovingly called me Simon Legree whenever I gave them very difficult assignments! No matter what we did on the field, they all knew that I loved them, and I still do. I still attend class reunions of the classes I taught during the 1950s. Seeing my former students as adults, with good families and successful careers, gives me the most wonderful feeling, for I can see in them the whole purpose of my having been a teacher.

At the time I began my teaching career in Cranford in 1949, I got the urge to play football again and agreed to be the quarterback for the Cranford Clippers, a semi-pro team that was in the Union County Football Conference. We had a great deal of fun on Saturday nights and Sunday afternoons playing teams from around the county and the state. We played a team from Staten Island too. At the end of the season, we defeated the team from Summit, New Jersey, in a very hard fought contest for the Union County Championship. That championship game ended my football playing days. When I reflect upon it, perhaps I was not very smart to play in those games when I had just begun my teaching career. I could have had career-threatening injuries. Funny, how youth has a way of re-ordering priorities and rationalizing away decisions that give serious credence to life down the road.

By 1954, through serious dedication to my job, I had worked up to being the head of the Social Studies Department. I was supervising a program involving ten regular teachers and a group of practice teachers from Rutgers and Montclair State College. During those years, I enjoyed a variety of assignments. I was in charge of the Student Council, worked on curriculum committees, coordinated the school's citizenship education program with Columbia University, and supervised the recreation program of the municipal playgrounds in the summer.

In January 1953, Judge Libby E. Sachar, the judge of the Juvenile and Domestic Relations Court of Union County, ap-

Jim Avery, second from right, being sworn in by Judge Libby Sachar along with other members of the Committee

pointed me chairman of the Cranford Juvenile Conference Committee. Such township committees were set up based upon Judicial Rule 6:2-2A which was adopted by the New Jersey Supreme Court. It was our job to meet monthly and to make a special study and investigation of each juvenile offender referred to us by the court. In each instance we sought to look at all the social and environmental circumstances that surrounded the young offender, such as the living conditions in the home, the level of parental discipline, and the nature of the action that drew enforcement attention. It was important to measure all of that against the offender's attitude, the reasons involved in the offense, and the ways to get the person back on track to complete his education and stay out of trouble.

I loved all aspects of my involvement in education. I especially liked the fact that I had the students who were going to top-flight colleges and universities like Princeton, Rensselaer Polytechnic, University of Pennsylvania, and Carnegie Mellon. I recall the special project on citizenship that earned TV recognition for my students. The Citizen Education Project, headquartered at Columbia University, was interested in increasing student participation in community service activities. The students completed a traffic survey in downtown Cranford and presented a revised parking plan that was accepted by the town council for implementation. The class was invited by a television station to go to Newark, New Jersey, where they taped a special TV show on the project. The students had a great time and felt like young TV stars. The people of Cranford were extremely proud of their students.

I felt strongly about the need to include citizenship training in my teaching and took steps to do so whenever possible. I never realized that this would get the attention of others in Cranford and in the state. One editorial in the local newspaper, the *Cranford Citizen and Chronicle*, praised this work as follows:

> It would be easier for the educators to forget the whole subject and leave the job of teaching America's heritage to other educational means which are probably less effective. Fortunately for the students of Cranford, our local school system has not taken the easy way. A real attempt is being made to make citizenship training a part of the total curriculum. While the emphasis of the study is in the Social Studies courses—such training—not always obvious—is going on in many types of study.
>
> Most of the citizenship training in the local school system is now emphasized in the high school under the leadership of James Avery, social studies teacher. For his efforts he has been praised by the administrators and the Board of Education. In this work, Mr. Avery has been ably assisted by many members of the faculty.
>
> For its work in educating students in the American way of life, the high school has been awarded the George Washington Honor Medal of the Freedom Foundation. Among things cited by the school in its entry were an article on the school store, a booklet produced by the seventh grade on the Township of Cranford, an account of the survey on parking made by the students, and pictures of the use of voting machines in student council elections.

During all of this educational activity, I married again in 1954 to Margaret Nunn from Summit, New Jersey. I first met her when a mutual friend, Joan Lambert, brought Margaret over to the high school one day. She was a beautiful girl who looked somewhat like the actress Dorothy Dandridge. We began going out on dates and, after a year or so, decided to marry. Margaret was a fun person with a wonderful personality that complemented her beauty. We bought a home in Plainfield, New Jersey, on George Street. The next year we had our first child and named her Sheryl. We did not want to use the letter C; we wanted to be a bit different and used the letter S to start her name. (Everyone calls her Sheri now.) We had a second child in 1958, and we named him after me, James S. Jr. Sheryl was and still is a very intelligent person. As a little one, I gave her all the records of songs and stories for tots. I loved to see her playing with them and singing the songs. She even wrote a little movie script in which she starred along with Jim in some backyard antics. Sheryl is a very talented person with both managerial and leadership qualities. She has a wonderful sense of humor and an infectious laugh. Sheryl grew up to be a wonderful mother and was involved in PTA activities in the schools her two children attended. I will never forget the poem she recited about her daughter Kelly at the Cambridge School in Kendall Park, New Jersey, Sixth Grade Farewell Celebration. (The children were being promoted into the seventh grade in a different school in the community.) Sheryl entitled it:

FAREWELL MY SIXTH GRADER

I have sat in the audience, the classroom,
watched from behind curtains and cupped hands.
I have been the applause, the exhausted resource center,
hunter of sharp pencils and metric rulers.
I've covered books with bags and baked cookies and cupcakes,
dressed you, combed you and kissed you goodbye.
It's always been more than the cuts and the bruises,
that 70 on the math test, the "oops, I forgot to tell you I
need a bag lunch for tomorrow," and "no, I can't wear
that today, I have gym."
It's watching you change right before my eyes that amazes me, scares me.
Seeing you close one door, as you ready yourself to open another seems
to leave me in the shadow of your childhood, for just awhile.
Just long enough to miss you already and maybe to cry, just a little.

It's an exciting kind of sadness, like it was running
beside your bike holding the seat.
Waving my pride and confidence as you pulled away
on two wheels for the very first time.
Every night I am hugging you, praying for you,
encouraging you, there are no limits to your
achievements, no mountains too high.
Keep your mind and body clean and prepared for the
challenge.
I wish you much luck next year in the seventh grade
And continued success for the rest of your life.

That poem was just an example of her talent to write and to speak. Today, Sheryl is managing a very busy Orthopedic practice in New Brunswick, New Jersey.

Jim, Jr. was a typical boy when growing up. He loved sports, including basketball, baseball, and especially golf. He went out for Junior High football, but after several rather hard tackles while carrying the ball, he felt that he enjoyed that game more as a spectator. I think he loved golf the best. It seemed to come naturally to him. I loved to play the different courses with him and beam as his drives went like rockets far down the fairway. Jim was good enough to be selected to play in the New Jersey Juniors Golf Tournament. He did not win, but he did very well, in coming in third overall.

During the early seventies, Margaret and I began to have serious marital problems. Differences in interests, in what we each felt was important in life, in attitudes about marriage, all had become far more overt once we moved from a home on Monroe Avenue in Plainfield to one on Inverness Drive in Scotch Plains, New Jersey. We Averys integrated Inverness Drive when we moved there. I thought Margaret handled that situation very well but in hindsight I do question whether the move was a good one socially. It may have been an environment that she accepted but never really wanted to be a part of. At the time,

I was travelling a lot for my company, and I admit that didn't help for a close family relationship, nor did it ease the living conditions for her. I was also very much involved in leadership roles in my fraternity, Omega Psi Phi. The added absences from home simply magnified the problems. The big differences in the things we liked to do loomed larger and larger.

One evening in 1972 after what seemed like months of discord, I came home to find that Margaret had moved out of our house, into an apartment in North Plainfield, leaving me to raise two children, who were then 16 and 13. Naturally, I was in a complete state of shock. She was determined not to come back. After an unsettling period of adjustment, I had no other recourse but to file for separation. After the separation, I had to depend a great deal on my sister Alice and my brother's daughter, Sandra, to stay with the kids when I was away on a business trip. I don't know what I would have done without their help. Four years later, Margaret initiated the divorce. It must be said, and I appreciate the fact, that in later years Margaret was very supportive of Sheryl, Jim, and their children; however, it was very difficult for both the children and me in the years immediately after Margaret's leaving us.

Getting back to my years of teaching at Cranford High in the fifties, all things were going well with my teaching position, my coaching, and the other assignments. I was set to be there for life. The Cranford-Kenilworth Junior Chamber of Commerce awarded me their Young Man of the Year Award in 1955 for the things I was doing in the community. The *Cranford Chronicle* had a flattering editorial on the award:

YOUNG MAN OF THE YEAR
INSPIRING EXAMPLE FOR YOUTH

> Although not presently residing in Cranford, James S. Avery, social studies teacher and athletic coach at Cranford High School, will be feted as "Young Man of the Year" by the Cranford-Kenilworth Chapter, Junior Chamber of Commerce, at a dinner tonight, is a product of our community and its school system. A native of Cranford, he resided here until moving to Plainfield

Plainfield Courier News
N.J. JAN 12 1956

James S. Avery
Honored by Jaycees

Jaycees Honor Local Teacher

a year ago and is a graduate of Cranford High School where he was active in athletics and also served as president of the Student Council and as "mayor" during the Boys' Week program sponsored annually by the Cranford Rotary Club.

The winning personality, which has made him so popular among fellow teachers and students alike, is Mr. Avery's own, but the town in which he was raised and the schools in which he spent his formative years also can take credit for an assist of the character which has made Mr. Avery the successful man that he is. Thus, the community at large can take justifiable pride in the honor conferred upon him.

In the nomination for the Jaycee accolade, Mr. Avery was cited for his service as faculty adviser of the Cranford High School Student Council, as leader of the school's citizenship program, and as athletic coach. In these roles he is closely associated with the youth of our town and exerts a powerful influence in the molding of the characters of our future citizens.

The extent of his influence is measured by the fact that, whether in the classroom or the athletic field, the students look up to him as a mentor they can both like and respect and as a living example of the worthiness of the precepts of the citizenship and sportsmanship he is teaching them. The factor of the good example being set for young people by Mr. Avery is stressed frequently in the "Young Man" nomination report, in which, for instance, he is commended for playing "a leading role in creating better race relations in Cranford and especially in the high school... through example rather then direct action." Again, in commending him for his work as sports supervisor for the municipal playgrounds, the report states: His well-organized programs of leagues and other competitions helped keep many Cranford children active and out of trouble. Here again, he helped to foster good race relations by setting a good example at all times for the children to follow.

Through example and education, in connection with his duties as Student Council adviser, Mr. Avery also was influential in the discouragement of wearing blue jeans to classes in the high school, an accomplishment which received wide recognition because it came about through persuasion rather than the banning action taken in some other school systems.

In addition to his present example as their teacher, Mr. Avery's students also can take inspiration from his own well-rounded program as a student at Cranford High School and Columbia University, including active participation in student affairs and sports in addition to conscientious attention to studies leading to bachelor of arts and master's degree.

His record also includes service to his country in the Army Air Corps and to his community in such roles as membership in the Civil Defense police reserves and the

> Community Council and Chairmanship of the Juvenile Conference Committee.
>
> In view of his past and continuing program of accomplishments, the endorsement of his personality by Cranford High School students in voting him the most popular teacher in the school, and the distinguished service award conferred on him by the Cranford Kenilworth Chapter, Junior Chamber of Commerce, Mr. Avery would seem a logical candidate for further "Young Man of the Year" honors on state and even national levels.

Earlier in the same week at an evening meeting of the local Parent-Teacher Association, I was presented with a state PTA Life Membership pin and a certificate which read: "In recognition of his interest and support in the work of the association."

In the 1950s, I had a young family and the accolades were well received by my wife, her family, and my own. It was fellow blacks in Cranford who expressed great appreciation for what they felt I had done, and it was a special kind of blessing to know they felt that way.

It seemed I was living the good life, ready to spend the remainder of my days teaching young people. Little did I know at the time that my life was soon going to change drastically.

In mid-December, 1955, I got a telephone call from an assistant manager of Esso Standard Oil Company's Public Relations Department. He said that Esso needed a professional Negro employee with a background in education and experience in community service who could function in the company's educational relations and race relations programs. His name was George A. Lloyd. He was the father of one of my students, Joan Lloyd. Apparently, Joan had suggested me to her father when he had mentioned that Esso was looking for such an individual. He wanted me to do this in Esso's 18 state operating territory in the U.S., a territory that ran from Maine to Louisiana. Well, I told him I would think about it. After all, it was a sudden shock to my system and to my pattern of living and working. I was happy in the field of education and I especially enjoyed helping young people shape their careers and develop their lifetime goals. Frankly I was not immediately interested in changing job directions, even though I knew that opportunities for further advancement were quite limited for blacks. I studied the opportunity, went deeply into the company's background, and finally decided that such a job was indeed a real challenge as well as a great chance to realize a lot more for both my family and me. So, in April of 1956, a few days after receiving the life membership from the New Jersey Congress of Parent-Teacher Associations and one day before being named "Young Man of the Year—1955" by the area Chamber of Commerce of Cranford and Kenilworth, New Jersey, I turned in my resignation effective at the end of the 1956 school year. In my letter of resignation I said, "In arriving at my decision, I felt that I must consider more than the present. I must think of even greater opportunities that are provided by this new post."

My teaching associates gave me a delightful and heartwarming send off. In my thank you that afternoon to them, I said:

> I cannot explain with any degree of adequacy the importance of my relationship with you these past seven years. Each one of you has played a significant role during my tenure here, no matter how small the part you may think it has been. When I look back and recall this present era, it shall be my associates that I shall review first and foremost with the greatest amount of respect and appreciation. Thank you most sincerely for the wonderful gift and your many kindnesses. I shall cherish both always.

Howard R. Best, the Superintendent of Schools in Cranford responded to my resignation in a letter of April 20, 1956, said:

> I received your letter of resignation and with a great deal of regret have presented it to the Board of Education. They followed your request and accepted your resignation as of June 30, 1956. We appreciate the fine work which you have done in the Cranford schools, the loyalty and cooperation which you have exhibited at all times throughout the years as a member of our staff. Our best

wishes go with you in this new experience which you will soon be entering and may it indeed be rich and fruitful as you continue through the years.

Sincerely,
H. R. Best

IX

Entering the Business World

I made the change to Esso Standard Oil Company on July 2, 1956, and in my new position would work chiefly in race relations and in the educational and civic fields. I had the same intentions as when I entered teaching in 1949, to commit myself wholehearted to every endeavor always doing the best that I could.

One may wonder what are some of the keys that opened various doors in my life to this point? There were many. I had a mother who was determined that I was going to get a college education. I had a father who showed me by example the meaning of responsibility by working day and night and doing anything that was respectable hard work to support his family. Both parents gave me a strong sense of self worth. I had teachers who never let me got bogged down in the frustration and defeatism that gripped many young black persons in those days. And, I had some good training in some sound Christian values that formed the basic moral foundation influencing all that I did.

I remember being interviewed that first day at Esso by Robert Scholl, executive vice president. He asked me, "What do you think you can do for us?" Some words came out of my mouth that seemed to make sense. I said, "Like any new member of the team, I have to learn the 'play book' and then I'll let my actions speak for themselves. Frankly, I want to be the best employee you got!" After I left his office I felt the enormity of the comment I had made about seeking to be one of the best black men in Corporate America.

At the time I joined Esso, there was one other black person involved in Esso's Negro Relations. His name was Wendell

P. Alston, a very distinguished gentleman who had come up through the ranks to his present job. He had been working in public relations with a man named James "Billboard" Jackson, who was the first black hired by Esso in a classified job level. This occurred in 1934 when the company pioneered the placement of a Negro representative in the Advertising and Sales Promotion Department. Billboard was one of the first (if not the first) black to work in a white-collar job for any major corporation. Billboard's nickname came from his previous work with Variety Magazine. Before that, Billboard had been a barker in a circus. As a part of the Advertising and Sales Promotion Department, Billboard was assigned to the sales promotion group that was advertising the new material to be used in tires, butyl rubber. He went around the marketing territory talking with minority groups about this new product for Esso tires. Butyl rubber came from an invention associated with a German inventor, I. J. Forman. I never learned very much concerning the story about Butyl rubber during the early phase of World War II. There was some PR problem that was linked to this special rubber and its origin involving Germany and that is why the Esso representatives went all over the marketing territory encouraging people to think well of butyl rubber.

During his years with Esso, Billboard was responsible for making the name Esso a well-known brand among "Negroes" (so called during that era) in America. He spent more than 50% of his time traveling through the company's marketing territory, particularly in the southern divisions. He made personal contact with business, professional, fraternal, religious, and educational groups in every major city. At a time when the pace of the socio-economic advance of the Negro was gaining momentum, these groups were eager for the kind of information Billboard was prepared to give them. He was in constant demand as a speaker at numerous gatherings and attended every annual convention held yearly by black organizations. Billboard took an active part in the conventions of major Negro organizations such as the Elks, Masons, Shriners, the National Negro Business League, the National Medical and Dental Associations, National Insurance Association, the National Negro Publishers Association, the National Funeral Directors

Association, ,and the National Beauticians Association. In fact, he was a member or an honorary member of every Negro national organization of any importance. This varied contact provided an excellent opportunity to evaluate the market potential of the Negro consumer, as well as, to create and nurture a favorable attitude towards our company, its products and its services.

Billboard was also responsible for Esso's use of a travel booklet *The Green Book* published by the Green Publishing Company. The South was still segregated, and *The Green Book* listed all the places that blacks could stop while traveling in the South without being denied service, be it food, gasoline, or accommodations. It included the Esso service stations where they could get service and use the bathrooms without being turned away. This booklet, during the height of prejudice and segregation in America, was a valuable item, and most blacks traveling through the southern states had it in the glove compartment of their cars.

When I was giving presentations for Esso during the late 1950s, I often had to stay in seedy, rundown hotels because I was not allowed to stay in a room or eat my meals in the major hotels in the South. I knew from personal experience how valuable *The Green Book* could be to black people in those days. *The Green Book* was like a security blanket that helped to sell Esso to the Negro community all across our marketing territory.

I thoroughly disliked it whenever I experienced segregated conditions. I never felt I was an inferior person or one whose intelligence level was lower than someone else. Being judged only for my skin color riled the hell out of me, but I was representing a major corporation, and I had to deal with it. In doing so it simply reinforced my feeling of self and strengthened my perception of who I was.

Billboard Jackson was a true pioneer in American corporate life, a man who really paved the way for other blacks to follow. I regret never knowing Jackson when he was in his prime, for I met him during the onset of his life-altering illness. He would make his way from his Harlem home to our offices every once in a while, but his language was very muddled and the words never made much sense. I felt deeply sorry for him.

The Public Relations Department of Esso Standard Oil Company put out a brochure with pictures and biographic information announcing its new Public Relations team that would be handling its Negro Relations program. Thousands of copies of the new brochure went to groups, organizations, and associations throughout the company's marketing territory, focusing principally on the South, where the anticipated benefit would be greatest.

I went into this new life with a strong feeling of confidence. I was in a completely new environment, working with a completely new group of people on a completely different set of objectives. I was now a commuter and with newspaper in hand I took the train to Jersey City, the ferry cross the Hudson River to New York, , and then the subway up to our mid-town office at 15 West 51st Street. I was not bringing work home as I did when I was a teacher. Evenings, when I was not traveling, were open for playing with the growing children and the weekends for social life with friends and relatives along with doing the necessary yard work at our home on George Street in Plainfield.

X

Becoming an Omega Man

Wendell P. Alston was a graduate of Johnson C. Smith and was also a member of the Omega Psi Phi Fraternity, Inc. It was because of him and other fraternity members who lived near me in Plainfield that I became a member of that fraternity. I was living on George Street at the time and three members of Omega Psi Phi lived close to me. Raymond Cruse, who had attended West Virginia State College, was a clerk with Mobil Oil in New York City, and was a devoted member of the fraternity. Ray lived just around the corner from me. Bill McKnight lived two houses from me on George Street and Donald Van Blake lived two doors from me on the other side. Don and Bill, like Ray, were fine college-trained Omega men, gentlemen in all respects, good fathers, good neighbors, and great guys to know. Further up on George Street lived Washington Nelson and his son Joel, two more Omega men, well known in the community and involved in civic life in Plainfield. So I was surrounded by "Ques," which was the nickname for Omega men. My family and I were friends with these men and their families before I knew they were members of Omega. It was Ray Cruse who first started talking to me about the fraternity on a commuter train heading to New York City. I was intrigued. When I attended Columbia College, there were no minority fraternities on campus, so I knew nothing about black fraternities or the depth of their concern for youth and social service or the fact that you could join their graduate chapters. Black fraternities had undergraduate chapters at colleges and universities, and graduate chapters chartered in various cities in America.

In 1956, I was asked by Ray and Donald to think about accepting an invitation to join the Omicron Chi Chapter, the graduate chapter in the Plainfield area. They gave me some material to read about the organization and its objectives.

Important motivators for joining an organization of men are the friendship and mutual respect among the members, and I saw these characteristics in casual situations, in organized social occasions and on a one-to-one basis as well. I respected these men and having them as neighbors made it even better. While I saw the examples my friends evinced, I experienced a larger view while traveling through the South with Wendell Alston, also an Omega man. Wherever we traveled in segregated areas and needed accommodations, Omega men helped provide them. If we needed contacts, Omega men helped provide them. No matter the occasion or the need, all Wendell had to do was to call his Omega brothers. It was a network of college men linked by a bond of friendship, mutual interests, and mutual respect. I liked this common interest among men and the idea of an unbreakable bond of friendship. I loved the idea of using talents and advanced training to help the less fortunate, to motivate others to attain higher goals in education, and to make a positive difference in a community. I was already trying to do this in my community life and here was an organization of men who had similar ideals of citizenship.

I learned that the fraternity was structured on four basic cardinal principles: manhood, scholarship, perseverance, and uplift. These principles are supposed to give fundamental support to a brother's behavior in everything he does in life. Manhood suggests that men of Omega must always be men of dignity, responsibility, and high character. Perseverance represents a determination to stay the course in seeking the highest and best purposes in all endeavors in life. Scholarship, the accumulation of knowledge and intelligence, is a goal that Omega men must always respect, reward in others, and seek themselves in educational attainment. Uplift is the principle in life that commands one to keep Christianity foremost in all he does.

In early 1957, I agreed to accept the invitation to join the Omicron Chi Chapter of the Omega Psi Phi Fraternity, Inc. While the practice of hazing was carried on through the years by similar organizations, particularly in the undergraduate chapters, I was glad that the Plainfield chapter did not agree with the idea of hazing or brutality in any form. I had expressed my concern about this, and that I was not interested in any organization that felt they had to use some kind of physical duress to initiate new members. It never made intelligent sense to me to abuse a man for any reason outside of the law, especially one whom you wanted to be lifelong friends with. You would think that the memory of the torture our forefathers went through as slaves would make any intelligent person abhor doing anything that reminded us of those tragic days in history.

Near the end of the summer of 1957, I went through the beautiful ceremony that made me an Omega brother. The Omicron Chi Chapter was chartered as a graduate chapter in 1955. I was the first person to be initiated into the chapter since it was chartered. It was a great honor for me, and it was a historical event as well. I will never forget the beautiful sight of the fraternity's shield bathed in candlelight and the countenance of Brother Ermon K. Jones, Omega's Second District Representative, who performed the ceremony, looking down upon me.

Brother Avery (front row center) with members of Omicron Chi, circa 1960

I loved being a member of Omega Psi Phi Fraternity, Inc. I involved myself in every aspect of the programs carried out by the Plainfield Chapter: the meetings, the scholarship activities, the Founders Days, and district and national affairs. After three years in the fraternity, I was elected Basileus (president) of Omicron Chi and led the chapter in successfully carrying out the programs and projects mandated by the national body. I also participated in the affairs of the Second District as Public Relations Director.

The fraternity was organized nationally into 12 districts, and ours, the Second District, composed of New York, New

Jersey, Pennsylvania, Delaware, and Maryland, was one of the largest and most important. I moved up from District Director of Public Relations to the position of District Representative in the next three years. Omega Psi Phi Fraternity, Inc., with over one hundred thousand members, was destined to be a very significant part of my life.

No one could be prouder of the fact that I had joined the Omega Psi Phi Fraternity, Inc. than Wendell, and as we traveled throughout Esso's marketing territory, I felt that same pride from other fraternity brothers.

Wendell had an interesting family. His half brother was Romere Beardon, a world famous collagist. His brother, Charles "Spink" Alston, was also a prominent artist who taught at the Metropolitan Museum of Art. Lena Horne, the beautiful movie star and outstanding vocalist, was related to him. Wendell had two sisters. One of his sisters was married to an opera star named Larry Winters, who spent most of his time singing in opera houses in Europe. Wendell himself was a fine artist, something I never knew until after his death when I saw some of his fine artwork. He was a distinguished man. He never cursed. He never raised his voice or argued. You might define him as just a fine, gracious gentleman. His wife, Helen, a retired teacher, had health problems and never wanted Wendell to be too far away from home. She always complained when we had to leave for a trip south.

When Wendell's mother died, the funeral was at Campbell's Funeral Home on Madison Avenue in New York City. This was a rather prestigious funeral home, for one would often read in *The New York Times* of very prominent people having funerals there. Wendell's family belonged to that middle-upper class of light-skinned blacks whose children went to summer camps and as adults were members of social organizations like the Nordsmen, Jack and Jill, and the Links. The day of the funeral for Wendell's mother at Campbell's I met some very famous blacks, several of them among the world's finest artists.

XI

Participating in Plainfield's Civic Life

Jim Avery, Chairman of Plainfield's Local Assistance Board, reviews welfare matters with Dr. Richard Cohen, Board Member, Ruth Dudley, Executive Director of the Welfare Department, and Board Member Anthony Sabino

In 1958, I was elected to the Board of Trustees of the Union County Psychiatric Clinic and served for several years as its Personnel Committee Chair. Based in Plainfield at that time, the Clinic, with its outstanding medical staff, was a very effective organization in helping to cure serious mental problems, particularly of young people in the county. At the same time, I was also asked to be a member of the Evening School Council to oversee the adult education activities in the city.

In 1960, the mayor of Plainfield, Richard Dyckman, approved by resolution of the Common Council, appointed me to the city's

Jim Avery, in one of his many meetings on civic affairs with Plainfield's Mayor Robert Maddox

Local Assistance Board, which was responsible for managing the welfare department in the city. I served on that board for eight years and was its chairman for the last four. Working with the welfare staff, we reduced the welfare rolls in the city to those who rightfully deserved assistance and cleared out those who could work but had been playing the system and living on the city's money.

In August 1963, Mayor Robert C. Maddox appointed me as a charter member of the newly established Human Relations Commission. At the Commission's organization meeting, I became a member of the Public Relations Committee and chairman of the Commission's Housing Committee. The first agenda item of the Housing Committee was to study the problem of substandard housing and to look into block-busting real estate activity. I asked Msgr. C. B. Murphy from St. Bernard's Catholic Church in the city to be my co-chairman for this important assignment. Studying substandard housing was not going to be very difficult because I immediately requested copies of ordinances and amendments regarding the subject along with those portions of the meeting minutes of the Department of Public Works that dealt with the situation. I also asked for information regarding the NAACP Housing Committee activities. The hard part would be the matter of block-busting.

Whenever blacks moved into white areas, whites began to move out. The problem was based upon the history of prejudice and segregation and the perceptions of many white citizens. There were realtors, both black and white, who took advantage of fears and perceptions of lower property values. In a concerted effort to ease the situation, we met with neighborhood groups in various parts of the city and helped form housing groups that supported the idea of integration. We participated as speakers in a number of public programs. One article in the *Plainfield Courier* in May 1964 told about an anti-bias program that I participated in at a Fellowship Day Program. One paragraph from the article stated:

> Avery, who is a public relations representative with Humble Oil & Refining Company *[Esso Standard was*

absorbed into Humble in the early 1960s], said, "Problems involved in freedom of residence have their basis not in legislation or court mandates but within ourselves." He said present progress in income, education, and expanding opportunities will lead to a steady demand for better homes and neighborhoods. He said that the Human Relations Commission was instrumental in developing one of two local neighborhood associations working together for interracial harmony in Plainfield. He cited a need to eliminate existing discriminatory practices in tenancy in housing projects, and said some cases have been referred to the state division of Civil Rights. His committee also helps prevent the spread of "blockbusting" tactics used by some real estate dealers and cooperates with the current revising of the local property maintenance code. "All of us," he declared, "should share in this responsibility to attain freedom of residence and to be better citizens and better Christians in our community."

That year Esso Standard Oil Company's magazine carried a major story on my activities in civic life, particularly as they related to the City of Plainfield.

The new charter is discussed (left to right) by local president Westry Horne, C. Chandler, State Representative for the Frontiers, Jim Avery, Vice President of the new chapter, and Jim King, Regional Vice President for Frontiers.

I was a charter member of the city's chapter of Frontiers International Inc., a public service organization like the Kiwanis, Lions, and Rotary Clubs except it was a black organization. I had been a member of the Newark, New Jersey, chapter of Frontiers International but transferred to the Plainfield Chapter when we organized it. While there were a number of local social problems in which the club was involved, the main national project was to focus attention upon a disease called sickle cell anemia. This condition occurs almost exclusively in people of African descent. It effects one in every 1,000 black persons. It is a disease in which a person has no normal hemoglobin in the red blood cells because of having inherited a sickle cell gene from one of the parents. In 2005, the problem of sickle cell anemia still exists but due to greater awareness and testing before marriage, the incidence is not as great as back in the 1960s when Frontiers International was spreading the word about the disease. During this period the Plainfield chapter became a recognized force in the black community. I was privileged to serve a term of office as the chapter's president. In April 1969, we hosted the annual community service award dinner of the Inter-Service Clubs of Plainfield, New Jersey. I served as the Master of Ceremonies when we presented the Plainfield Community Service Award to an outstanding community leader named Reverend Harold Husted.

Jim Avery of the Plainfield, New Jersey Chapter of Frontiers International presents the "Man of the Year" award to Reverend Harold Husted, 1969

As an Esso representative, I attended many of the Frontier International regional and national meetings, served on several committees, and was the secretary of the organization's national Youth Service Committee. After being president for two terms and moving out of Plainfield, I no longer remained active with Frontiers International, which is continuing today as an active part of Plainfield's community life.

Jim Avery, right, after receiving a Frontiers International Award at the organization's 1966 Convention in New Orleans, Louisiana

XII

Education and Race

I don't know whether it was due to my joining Esso or the attention the media drew to my various civic appointments, but I began to get invitations to speak at meetings of various clubs and organizations. This was particularly true when I visited various cities in the Esso Standard operating area. While on my first trip to Louisiana, I appeared before the Rho Phi Chapter of the Omega Psi Phi Fraternity, the Frontiers International Club in New Orleans, business groups in Alexandria, Louisiana, and the business students at Southern University in Baton Rouge.

I gave a number of talks in the local Plainfield area too, starting with a Laymen's Sunday service program at the Bethel Presbyterian Church. My speech to the Council of World Friendship on "The Changing Status of the Negro" drew attention to the need for more black inclusion in the overall affairs of American life.

The first speech I made after joining Esso, which was later printed and circulated, was in May of 1958 when I spoke to the members and guests of the Elizabeth Kiwanis Club at the Luerich Foundation Awards Luncheon. My topic was, "Important Foundations for the Development of Good Citizenship." The program was widely attended by Elizabeth educators, clergy, business people, and youth, and the Kiwanis found it so timely that they printed and distributed the speech. At the ending part of the talk I said:

> Well, you may ask, what is the remedy? [For the need for developing foundations of behavior and of putting them into practice before real citizenship can become a reality.] What are the magic words that will solve all

> our problems and bring us this Utopia in citizenship? Seriously, as parents we cannot expect to eliminate all problems any more than we can eliminate the people who cause them. But we can do a great deal to bring about considerable improvement. Basically, we must provide the climate where young people can develop the characteristics for self-respect, self-reliance, and respect for the rights and property of others. This kind of environment must give them the opportunities they need to work out their problems and make up their own minds about decisions which bear upon the province of youth. Youngsters need greater opportunities to develop their innate capabilities, and a sense of their own responsibilities. They need guidance in developing a respectable code in the right way to live and the best way to treat their fellow man.
>
> Throughout these formative years we must encourage each one to learn and understand the foundations and ideals of democracy. This is essential if we are to expect an unswerving devotion to the actions that democracy requires. These are the underlying needs that must become part of the character of youth if they are to develop a wholesome appreciation for the realistic practice of democratic and Christian ideals basic to good citizenship behavior. We have the responsibility—in fact, the obligation—to produce this kind of young American. How can each of us, in good faith, call ourselves citizens of this great country unless we do!

I thoroughly enjoyed my work as a civic leader in the community. All my life I felt driven to excel in representing my race in leadership roles in all aspects of community and corporate life. This was also to be true later in life when I held state, regional, and national positions.

This attitude was true of my work in Esso's Public Relations Department, which included several areas of importance to the company: race relations, dealer relations, press relations, educational relations, community relations, and counseling company management on activities that affect product sales and the company image. Wendell Alston and I enjoyed being responsible for the company's interface with black organizational life in Esso's marketing territory. This responsibility included our involvement in the operations and policy structure of black organizations. We made visits to educational institutions and community groups to motivate youth to higher educational aspirations. One of the activities I enjoyed most were my visits to business classes in various colleges and universities. J. A. Thomas, of the National Urban League, and I made several visits to Dr. Price's business classes at Delaware State. Both Wendell and I visited with Dr. W. O. Bryson's classes at Morgan State. I made a number of visits to meetings of the Business Club in Howard University's Department of Business Administration and arranged field trip itineraries for them. At that time, Professor Dr. H. Naylor Fitzhugh mentored the Business Club. In fact, the Business Club at Howard in 1961 conferred on me the first honorary membership ever given to any business representative. Each year we also visited the business classes at Tennessee A&I University where Bill Harper and William Crump were on the staff.

Wendell and I were constantly on the go with one activity after another. We dispensed information on travel and accommodations for blacks, and we participated in communications and onsite meetings with black community leaders. One of the major objectives of these onsite meetings was to recruit blacks for Esso station dealerships. People talk about economic empowerment today as if it were a new idea. Back in the late 1950s we sought to bring some economic empowerment into the black community through service station management and ownership in major urban areas.

The company had excellent educational materials to help school children understand things like map reading, the binary system, colonial America, how oil was discovered, produced, refined, and marketed, and an explanation of various energy sources. We sought to make them available without cost to teachers in our marketing territory. There were teacher associations in most states, and we used them as major distribution points. Below the Mason Dixon line, the teacher associations were segregated. Wendell and I participated with other PR personnel in the conventions of the educational associations in the north and attended the black conventions separately in the south. Providing these free materials was an outstanding way to convey our company's strong interest in teaching and in education.

In 1958, our Public Relations Department produced a motion picture called "The Cranford Story." Esso singled out one town, my hometown of Cranford, to relate the broad story of industrial contributions to education. I helped provide the technical background, outlining what industry was doing to help teachers improve science instruction. It was an honor for me to present an official copy of the film to Cranford High School. The motion picture was used in various school systems, at educational conventions, and on educational television stations in the eastern part of the United States.

It was my view that industry-sponsored school programs have worn assorted badges of merit for a number of years and that they were a vital part of corporate citizenship and a boon to teachers. While their basic function hinged on good public relations, it has been said that such programs have good marketing value. However, this was a claim and no one had actually attempted to prove it. I developed a research project to seek the answer. It had two objectives: first to obtain further information on the effectiveness of providing educational materials in forming favorable attitudes toward the company, and second, to obtain some indication of the influence of such educational materials on the buying habits of teacher consumers.

The questionnaire gave the appearance of being an independent work of a former teacher interested in conducting a study that dealt with free industry-sponsored teaching materials. The paper and envelopes that we used, the mailing procedure, and the return address gave no indication that Esso or any company was involved. In the questionnaire, four large industry-programs for schools were researched. Teachers were asked if they knew of or had used the materials. They were asked about their attitudes toward the respective company and the factors that influenced their choice in the attitude and buying behavior question. The survey went to 1,746 teachers in our marketing region, mostly randomly selected from educational directories. Our response was 37% of the mailings, an unusually high number. Fifty-seven percent came from teachers who had requested our educational materials and 43% came from names randomly selected. The statistical results indicated that ESSO's school materials program was an unusually strong builder of favorable attitudes toward the company and an effective catalyst in bringing about the sales of our products. I circulated the result to our upper management with the proviso that these aids must always be sincerely provided and never appear as a conduit for advertising purposes, for that would create intense disfavor.

Esso Research & Engineering Company had a wonderful exhibit of the products that Esso developed and marketed using the theme that "Esso Works Wonders with Oil." There were many black groups like morticians, the Elks, bankers, insurance companies, teacher associations, and the black press that held annual national conventions. Wendell and I had the Research Company's exhibit shipped to the location of the particular convention, and he and I would set it up and talk about the various segments of it with convention attendees. We also gave out the Green Books mentioned earlier and little souvenirs like mirrors and leather key holders that had our names on them. In this fashion, we got to know major black leaders around the country. Whenever we visited a city in the South, we met with local leaders we had met at the various conventions, and we also visited the segregated junior and senior high schools. The principals of these schools were glad to have two black men who represented a major corporation visit the school. In several instances they actually stopped classes and convened assemblies on the spot so that we could talk to the students. Our general message was that the world was undergoing change and that opportunities would be there for them if they prepared themselves for it. We challenged them to get good grades and to have high aspirations. I enjoyed doing those special programs with the students in the South because I was talking with young black kids who needed to hear this information. I hoped it helped them learn that there was a world for them beyond the limits of segregation.

During this time, my dad went on another of his visits to see his sister Rosa Davenport in Petersburg, Virginia. He loved going back to where he was born. His half-sisters Louise and Elizabeth still lived there so he could see all of them. It was the summer of 1959 and he was in his eighty-sixth year. It was there that he had a stroke and was taken to the hospital in Petersburg. All of us, my brothers and my sister, converged on Petersburg to be at his side. The room he was in had a sign on it, "Danger: Oxygen being used inside." When we saw him, his upper body was in one of those plastic hoods that in those years was used to give patients oxygen. We knew then that his condition was extremely serious. He could not speak. We had never seen him in a hospital bed, and he looked so fragile lying there. He had always been an active, healthy, hardworking man. This new image was shocking to us. After several days with no real change in his condition, my brothers and sister Alice decided to go back to New Jersey to their jobs with plans to return on the weekend. I told them I was not going to leave Dad, and I called my manager at Esso to say I was going to remain in Petersburg. One night when I returned to the hospital, I could see my Dad gesturing under that hood. I could not understand his mumbling, and I lifted the end of the hood and found that the heat under it was intense. I raised hell on that floor, yelling at the nurses, the supervisor, even an orderly about why no one had checked him to realize that the oxygen device was not working properly. I left him late that night, and my dad died before I could return the next morning. We arranged to have him brought back to Cranford, New Jersey, for his funeral and burial in Fairview Cemetery not far from mother's grave. The night of dad's wake after everyone was gone and the lights in the church were turned off, I sat

John H. Avery, age 86

there next to him and only left him early the next morning to change my clothing for the funeral. I must have kissed him and cried by his side all night…just he and I together. After all, as he once said, I was his Baby Boy, his 180-pound son, and I loved him beyond all definition.

After my father's death, my life returned to a state of normalcy, and I continued my activities at Esso. An important phase of my responsibilities in public relations was to inform management on what I felt to be important aspects of race relations. I recall writing a memorandum in August of 1959 responding to a question from our regional management asking, "Are there new ways of approaching Negroes?" I said:

> My response to you is based upon census studies, on motivational research and, most important, my actual experience. In the past several years, the general school integration picture, economic boycotts, civil rights legislation, FEPC laws (equal protection) state anti-discrimination statutes and new population changes have had a marked effect on Negro status and attitude. We have pointed out through various studies that the Negro is involved in a great migration. He has left rural farm areas in great numbers for the economic attractions of the city. Within this shift is a noticeable internal movement toward improved income status. Like other groups before him, as the Negro becomes more financially able he moves into the nearer suburban areas. Such northern and now suburban population movement stimulated by higher income employment is bringing an increasing number of Negroes in contact with better education and has had a stabilizing effect on home ownership. This migration has brought him closer to whites in terms of personal values, resources for living, standards of living, and duration of life. With differences between whites and Negroes lessening in these areas, it is safe to assume that to be successful, certain Negro market programs will have to play down policies predicated upon differences. In some areas these programs must no longer be looked upon as Negro market activities.

It is somewhat different in the larger cities where the Negro is more concentrated and generally poorer in economic status. Disapproval of social and economic inequities is the cohesive force that nurtures racial pride and contributes to its intensity. In these areas discrimination is felt more keenly. While market programs can profitably continue to make direct reference to this group, such programs must appeal on the basis of liberal and progressive tact. If not, they do more harm than good. Internal changes in attitude and status are taking place. We can no longer assume that all Negroes act and think alike. We cannot approach the various classes of Negroes with the same programs, in the same way and expect the same result.

The Negro class structure contains several basic indications that can stand re-emphasis at this point. First, there are noticeable changes in attitude and behavior that accompany upward movement in class status. Secondly, for the most part, leadership is vertical in terms of class not in terms of race. Third, on an increasing basis, the level of one's intellect and social perspective is not necessarily related to their class status. Fourth, regardless of class, Negroes continue to take pride in the accomplishment of members of the racial group—especially when these activities transcend discriminatory barriers.

Our present public relations program is keyed to the middle and upper class Negro. We are not reaching the masses as effectively as we should. Since the masses are not well organized, little opportunity prevails for effective personal contact. Therefore, we recommend that mass media be used—specifically, the Negro press. The Negro press is virgin territory for good press releases about activities in which Negroes are involved in positive and favorable ways.

(At this time, with the exception of soft drinks, cigarettes, and alcoholic beverages, there was little corporate advertising directed toward blacks in the black press.)

We are marketing in an area where the Negro is becoming an increasingly important economic factor.

> Being in business to make a reasonable profit, we cannot ignore the implications. It will mean more concern all along company lines. For best results a program of orientation for company marketing personnel may be the answer. The procedure could be to set up division and district meetings—workshop like activities discussing the proper approaches and the kind of activities that will successfully attract his business.

This period, with the provision of counsel like this to our management, was the beginning of a number of effective changes in the way Esso dealt with its race relations. I presented numerous memorandums to top management relating to our Negro relations program. They included new ideas regarding educational relations, dealer relations, media relations, and employee relations, as well as, programs specifically directed to business, youth and women groups, and fraternal organizations. One of them, in 1962, pointed out the need to review our knowledge and interest in the so-called Negro market. I pointed out a number of factors that were relevant at that time. One was its growth potential. The Negro population in 1960 was increasing nationally at a rate almost 50% faster than whites. It was a young market with a median age of 23 versus that of 30 for whites. At the time, more than one-half of all Negroes lived within the 78 largest cities in the United States where nine-tenths of all wholesale sales and two-thirds of all retail sales are made. According to the U.S. Department of Commerce, Negro purchasing power had doubled from 1950 to 1960 and was expected to reach $27 billion by 1965. Home ownership had increased dramatically from 1960 to 1980 too.

The need to educate corporate management on race matters was amazing to me, for when I joined Esso they did not have that knowledge and did not appear to be interested in it. I had to present the information in a way that linked itself to sales in the marketplace and the good potential for profits. I knew that whenever you are talking to corporate management about consumer-oriented programs, the bottom line of profits or return on investment must always by the objective.

In 1959 external forces began to take shape that placed a major spotlight on the disparity between the purchasing power of blacks and the percentage and level of employment in firms where significant buying power was expended. One of the most effective of these forces was the Collective Patronage Campaign conducted by 400 Philadelphia ministers and led by Dr. Leon Sullivan. The campaign was effective in advocating the boycotting of products of companies that did not increase and upgrade black employment. The major products targeted at that time were soft drinks, breads, milk, and gasoline.

Fortunately, Esso was not boycotted partly because I had met personally with Dr. Sullivan and the ministerial group in Philadelphia and told them that we were in the midst of adding blacks to our clerical and sales force. I also took Esso's Regional Manager with me to another meeting with the ministers so they could hear it from him personally. Esso was not boycotted, but Gulf Oil and Sun Oil were among those that were. Gulf Oil quickly followed our lead and began hiring minorities for sales jobs.

Jim Avery (left) and three other members of Esso Standard Oil's public relations management team pose with ten newly hired black sales representatives at Rockefeller Center, NYC

During this time, I visited Philadelphia often and got to know many of the black leaders including ministers like Reverend Marshall Shepard, Jr., and Dr. Leon Sullivan. Marshall and I became great friends. Leon was pastor of the Zion Baptist Church on Broad Street and devoted a great deal of his time to encouraging blacks to become trained for the emerging job market. He founded the Opportunities Industrialization Centers of America where young men and women could get the training and skills needed for the job market. It was his "Sullivan

Principles" that structured the business guidelines for United States corporations operating in South Africa. He was a distinguished, widely known man with a persona of dignified strength. You just knew he was a man on a mission that had a great purpose for mankind.

When we became a part of Humble Oil & Refining Company, using the marketing name Humble, I had to go to Chicago, Illinois, in 1963 to defuse another ministerial boycott conducted by a militant organization known as the Negro Labor Relations League (NLRL). The League, first organized in 1935, had been successful through the years in combating the denial of fair employment to black citizens of Chicago. Picketing business locations, selective patronage, and street corner meetings were the principle methods used by this group. The Negro Labor Relations League was headed by Reverend M. Earle Sardon. The group circulated a bulletin entitled "A Fighting Crusade" with the names of companies that should be boycotted, and Humble's name was on the list. I spent several days holding meetings with our marketing management and various organizations. I met with Al Prejean, Associate Director of the Chicago Urban League, to discuss our employment picture and our desire to broaden our communication with other groups. I learned from Prejean of the formation of a community council of all responsible race oriented groups. The objective of this council was to coordinate the efforts of member groups, forcing them to use rational methods of approach and protest. Mr. Prejean agreed to communicate our discussion with this group. I also met with Balm Leavell, publisher of the *New Crusader* in Chicago, to discuss the Negro Labor League. He knew Reverend Sardon personally and arranged a meeting for me with the reverend. I held meetings with our service station dealers, some local business leaders, a number of customers picketing our stations, and with State Representative W. N. Robinson, a fraternity brother of mine and a political power on the Chicago South Side, to explain our business and our employment policies. I finally had a lengthy meeting with Reverend Sardon, who was very surprised that he was meeting with an executive of the company who also was a Negro! After the meeting with him and his aides he said, "We'll have to move Humble to the "trade with" column. From the next day on there were no pickets at our service stations. It was interesting that when my meeting with Reverend Sardon and his aides ended, they voiced great pride in the level of my responsibility and asked that I visit with them socially on my next trip to Chicago.

We had been caught napping in Chicago. Our management was fully cognizant of the need for more action, but the challenge of building a marketing organization had not put priority on black employment. Unfortunately, in that region, proper steps had not been taken to communicate to the black community the things that had already been done. I emphasized to top management, after that episode, that our efforts in the future in all cities should take the form of preventative medicine, and we should not find ourselves again in the position of finding the proper serum to head off the epidemic.

Boycotts of this kind, called Selective Patronage Campaigns, took place during those years in a number of other cities in our marketing region. Leaders of black communities in Memphis, New Orleans, Baton Rouge, Little Rock, Savannah, Raleigh, Durham, and Pittsburgh all had some boycotting activity going on. We were able to keep the company out of this negative limelight principally through the personal contacts we had developed over the years with the minority group leadership in those cities.

At that time in America no topic was receiving as much attention as that of civil rights for black people. Among whites, the subject was being discussed with attitudes ranging from complete indignation, to indifference, to outright support. Among blacks the feeling was best defined in the expression, "We want freedom now!" As I traveled in our region I heard that phrase echoing from poolrooms and barbershops to plush commercial offices, from the big city street corners to neat middle class homes in the suburbs. Mass demonstrations, and other successful pressure tactics, federal, state, and local legislation, Supreme Court decisions, and the support of numerous whites, had already helped crumble many of the barriers that beset blacks in seeking jobs, using public and private facilities, and obtaining equal education and finding housing.

Corporations, smaller businesses, all levels of government, and a variety of institutions in American life were confronted with this insistent cry for immediate, direct action to eliminate segregation and to bring about equal opportunity.

The company participated in several activities other than employee recruitment to manifest its interest in the minority community. Esso placed company deposits in black banks, advertised in the black press, and they developed plans for participation in a Small Business Administration's MESBIC. We continued to maintain direct contact with outside groups like the Urban League, NAACP, and Opportunities Industrialization Centers (O.I.C.), all effective in assisting us with employment leads. We also conducted a summer employment program in the region called Early Minority Identification Program (EMID). This activity provided meaningful jobs and exposure for a number of high potential minority men and women in colleges and universities in the region.

In the Northeastern Region, we were very aggressive in hiring black sales representatives for our marketing districts in New York, New Jersey, Pennsylvania, Delaware, and Maryland. Other companies like Clairol, Coca-Cola, Pepsi Cola, and Mobil Oil had hired representatives in the New York area. We eventually organized this group of sales representatives into a somewhat amorphous group of sales promotion, public relations, and marketing men called the Association of Market Specialists. I was elected president of the group and, through monthly luncheon meetings, sought to provide information relating to personality development, selling ideas, and up-to-date marketing techniques. This group was later absorbed into a national organization called the National Association of Market Developers, Inc.

No matter what we did it was extremely important to set a favorable sales climate for customers by giving members of the general public a positive image of the company, its people, and its products. We were in a very competitive market and a key objective was to get people who used petroleum products to choose our product over that of a competitor. As a member of company management who wanted the best for his company and a black man proud of his heritage, I felt the strongest kind of motivation to get and keep Esso on the right track.

While on my travels through the southern states of our marketing territory, I was disturbed by the small number of Esso service stations run by blacks in the black population centers. I saw that most of them were located in the rural areas and small towns. As a result, one of the first things I did was to research the location of the Esso service stations operated by blacks and, correspondingly, the location of the major centers of black populations. I was temporarily assigned to the company's research department to work on a survey with the Dickter's Motivational Research Company. Motivating consumers by various favorable themes to get them to express preference in attitudes and in their buying behavior was gaining in popularity. This temporary move was to give me a better understanding of the various aspects of the kind of research I was doing. It also helped in the early formulation of the advertising that we began in the publications of black organizations distributed at conventions. I thoroughly enjoyed that experience and when I had completed the research I could show that the service stations were, for the most part, not located anywhere near the centers of black population. In my view, we were not in a good position to be a competitive marketer and to take advantage of our standing in the black community.

I made a presentation of the findings to company management and recommended that Wendell and I visit the key cities where our stations were not located in or near minority population centers. The idea was to meet with key black leaders in these areas to explain the situation and request their help in finding qualified black persons who could become our dealers at company-owned service stations situated more closely to the centers of black population. The presentation also pointed out the significance of projecting our black dealers in such locations in an advertising campaign in black media. Top management approved the plan, but first I was sent to each sales district in the company's marketing territory to present the research program that I had completed with the recommended solution to the service station disconnect. I will never forget how I ended each presentation, knowing I was talking to white management. As I concluded, I said:

"Gentlemen, I am talking about ways to increase our customer base as well as the marketing presence of Esso in our operating territory. Let us never forget, it is not the black and white that counts, it's the green!"

In later years, members of management told me they still remembered that presentation and that last line about "The Green." It must have been effective because the project resulted in getting our stations where black people lived and increasing the number of black dealers running and owning Esso service stations. In the process, we got to know the leadership of all the various communities better and reinforced their positive image of Esso.

It was in 1960 that the Humble Oil & Refining Company, essentially a producing and refining company headquartered in Houston, Texas, and an Esso Corporation affiliate, took over Esso's marketing function in the United States. With this decision, the overall management of the public relations function was moved to Houston. Since we were now working with a company management that had little familiarity in dealing with minorities in this important aspect of human relations, I had to essentially re-invent the wheel to get management to understand race relations and its importance to the company.

Wendell Alston retired several years later and a young black employee named James Queen, a salesman in our Philadelphia District, joined me. James and I remained at Rockefeller Center in New York City working out of Houston. Since our activities moved to a nationwide level, I was made a national community relations coordinator and Jim worked under my supervision as a community relations representative. Fortunately, I had carte blanche to travel all over the United States. I was called upon by marketing managers to trouble shoot situations in many plant and office locations from one end of the country to the other. A major responsibility, however, was to educate top management at Humble about black America and to see that we adopted a more aggressive stance with our race relations activities.

Prior to Humble's assuming responsibility for our national marketing operations, Esso Standard Oil Company was a subsidiary of Esso Corporation. Esso could only market its products in the United States under the Esso name in the 18-state territory I mentioned earlier. This limited marketing was a result of a Supreme Court decision in 1911 when the Standard Oil Company of New Jersey had to relinquish its control over subsidiaries marketing under the Esso name in other states in the U.S. In the lower southeastern states, Florida, Georgia, and Alabama, Kentucky Standard Oil was the marketer. In Ohio, it was the Standard Oil of Ohio. Standard Oil products on the West Coast were marketed under the Chevron logo. When Humble took over the marketing responsibility, it opened up the door to market our products in a broader area under the Humble name and the brand name of affiliated companies like Pate Oil in Wisconsin and Gasateria in Indiana.

It was not until some ten years after the Humble takeover, that it was decided to seek one name that could be used to market our products throughout the United States. The brand name selected, which has no meaning in any language, was Exxon. The affiliated company responsible for marketing nationally was now called Exxon Company, U.S.A.

XIII

The National Association of Market Developers, Inc. (NAMD)

While working for Esso, I had the opportunity to be involved with other organizations, so in 1956 I became active in the National Association of Market Developers, (NAMD). It had been organized in 1953 as a national professional association of specialists in sales, advertising, marketing, and public relations directed primarily toward the development of the Negro market. NAMD, the only organization of its kind at the time, sought, through personal contact and the adoption of official policy, to raise the level of ethics and performance among Negro market practitioners. NAMD also sought to create and maintain a positive climate of opinion through positive communications with the press, community organizations, educational institutions, industry, and government. One of the most important objectives of the organization was to provide, through national conferences, regional meetings, and chapter activities, the exchange of information, experiences, and know-how by keeping members current on new sales techniques and vital information concerning the Negro market. NAMD was not a political or pressure-type group. Its function was wholly educational and professional. It was a non-profit organization, and its revenue was derived from membership dues.

I became the national president of the National Association of Market Developers, Inc., in 1963 at its tenth annual convention in Washington, D.C. At that conference we passed a resolution asking President Kennedy to direct U.S. businessmen to probe more deeply into the causes of Negro unemployment and to find solutions. The statement commended the president for his interest and concern with equal employment opportunities for Negro citizens. I was re-elected president at each of the next three annual conventions in 1964, 1965, and 1966. I became Chairman of the Board of NAMD for 1967.

The Board of Directors of the National Association of Market Developers, 1964. Jim Avery (front-row center) was the national president

In the spring of 1996, I wrote an article for *The Black Collegian* magazine entitled, "African-American Pioneers in the Corporate Sector." The article included information about black market specialists who helped to form the National Association of Market Developers. The article began as follows:

> African-American pioneers in the corporate sector 60, 50, and even 40 years ago blazed real trails in sales promotion, public relations, and marketing fields. They worked in a socioeconomic environment with vastly different conditions than those experienced by African-American business representatives today. With segregation and discrimination throughout the marketplace, the Black representatives, as few as they were, were severely limited in dealing with and marketing directly to the Black communities. In the early '30s, at the time of the very first Black Market representative, the Negro consumer market was an unknown quantity, practically nonexistent in the "marketing eyes" of American business. Few companies gave credence to or even believed that it was a clearly defined entity. The companies that were involved referred to what was then called the Negro Market as a special market and to the Black representatives they hired or

employed as "market specialists." White management had no idea who the Black community leaders were, or the organizations that existed therein, or what Blacks were doing other than the sensational things they read in the major media. Some companies saw this market as being so "special" they did not employ a Black to do the job, they made arrangements with a self-employed Black businessman to do the job for them. Working in only five consumer product areas (tobacco, petroleum, food, alcoholic beverages, and soft drinks), these outside representatives were like satellite units that represented the company at conventions and other meetings. They also provided marketplace intelligence to white management.

There was no organized recruitment program that included Blacks. The representatives selected were essentially handpicked. Making a choice of someone for this "special market" in this hand picked way was apparently a "safe way" for the companies to make the best start. Once hired these "special market" representatives had no formal company training, no course in sales promotion, merchandising methods or product development beyond that which was self-taught. Equipped only with a "do it yourself" kit, the Black marketer went forth like the veritable pied piper to create product awareness and Black consumers for the goods and services that were made available by the companies. They had expansive territories to cover, but no specific timetable or quotas to reach, no marketing plan from which to follow and no formal report to make. It was not unusual for anyone beyond the immediate boss or his secretary not to know at any time where the special representative was on any specified day. The special representative, being Black, knew the market well, its class structure, its customs, its organizations, and its consuming behavior. This was the principle reason for the success of these early marketplace pioneers who worked in what was considered a special market set-aside for specialized attention by a special representative.

> What major corporations at the time never accepted or seem to understand was the fact that the racial patterns they saw were actually responses in reaction to the behavior of members of the white community. The Negro market was not a creation of Negroes, it was a market created and defined by the many complex consequences of racial prejudice. The formation of NAMD was motivated by the need to improve the professionalism and specialized training of these special representatives who served that market.

I was very pleased that the publisher of *The Black Collegian* kept the complete article on their Web site under "African-American Issues" following its publication. I hope that many students at the black colleges and universities took the time to read it.

I thoroughly enjoyed my leadership role in NAMD and felt I did a great deal to expand the chapters and bring national leaders and major economic and business issues to our national conferences. Perhaps our finest annual national meeting was the 1964 conference held in Houston, Texas, where we had some of the finest speakers and panelists in their fields at the time. The banquet speaker was Representative Charles Diggs, who was a Congressman from Michigan. Among other key speakers were Dr. Andrew Brimmer, Deputy Secretary of U.S. Department of Commerce; Dr. Samuel Westerfield, Deputy Assistant Secretary for Economic Affairs U.S. Department of State; Bill Trent, an Assistant Director of *Time, Inc.*; and Mal Goode, American Broadcasting Company's news correspondent. All of these

1964 NAMD convention (left to right): Dr. H. Naylor Fitzhugh (Howard University), Cong. Charles Diggs (Michigan), Jim Avery, and C. B. Davis (local chapter president)

men were black leaders in their field. We gave awards to the United States Government's Plans for Progress Program, to Cummings Engine Company, an outstanding example of plans for progress at work, and to the American Association of Advertising Agencies for work it had done to combat discrimination in advertising.

Jim Avery (third from right), national president of NAMD, visits the Baltimore chapter

As national president of NAMD, I participated in a number of local chapter award banquets and other celebrated occasions, such as marketing clinics and career conferences. Most of my comments centered on encouraging youth to see the new opportunities that lie ahead in business and industry and encouraging more and more companies across America to keep pace with the advances of the times and accept a strong sense of social responsibility in their business ethics. News stories of my visits to the local NAMD chapters appeared in black newspapers that served many minority communities. Newspapers such as the St. Louis *Argus*, the St Louis *American*, the Oklahoma *Eagle*, the Atlanta *Daily World*, the Indianapolis *Recorder*, the Carolina *Times*, the *Carolinian*, the New Jersey, Baltimore, and Pittsburgh Afro-American newspapers, the Louisiana *Weekly*, the New York *Amsterdam News*, the Norfolk *Journal and Guide*, the Houston *Informer*, the Dallas *Express*, the Michigan *Chronicle*, and the Miami *Herald* all carried the stories repeatedly about our organization.

At that time, I had and still have the greatest respect for the leaders of the black press and the communications job they were doing. I knew John Stenstacke, publisher of the Chicago *Defender*, whose newspaper honored several of us in leadership roles in marketing, sales and public relations positions. John initiated the meeting in 1940 that led to the formation of the National Newspapers Publishers Association. The motivating idea was economic based. Stenstacke felt that by combining resources and buying materials in bulk they could save costs and generate increased advertising support. In my Esso travels I came to know many of the pioneering publishers of the time. I am referring to men like Carl Murphy of the Baltimore *Afro News*, Garth Reeves of the Miami *Herald*, C.C. Dejoie of the *Louisiana Weekly*, Louis Martin of the Michigan *Chronicle*, and Tom Young of the Norfolk *Journal and Guide*.

At this period in America's journalistic history, the black press was extremely important to the black community. Major daily newspapers did not report much news about black people except stories about murders or robberies. It was the black media that carried the stories of social events and the activities of the organizations and churches in the local community. The black press suffered from the fact that their circulation figures were low in comparison with the major newspapers, since most major advertisers were basing their ad placement solely on the newspaper's audit bureau's circulation that eliminated the black press from consideration. With the exception of some soft drink and liquor ads, the black press did not get major advertising and only got by because of advertising support from local black and white businesses. Esso Standard was just like other major companies with their advertising decisions, and I had a continuing major effort to get the company to ignore the circulation figures and realize that an important part of reaching the black community was to respect the importance of its media. Finally, in 1960, the company began to place advertising in black newspapers in our marketing territory, in magazines like *Ebony* and in the convention publications of major black organizations.

In 1967, my promotion to the position of Public Relations Manager for Esso Standard Oil's Northeastern Region coincided with the end of my tenure of three terms as president and one year as board chairman of the National Association of Market Developers, Inc. At the organization's 1967 National Conference in Houston, Texas, I expressed my deep feeling of respect and honor at being involved with this outstanding association from 1956 up to and including 1967. I still treasure the plaque presented to me by the incoming board chairman that year, who was my good friend, Dr. H. Naylor Fitzhugh,

James Avery, community relations coordinator with the Humble Oil and Refining Company, accepts a plaque for three years of service as president and one year as chairman of the board of the National Association of Market Developers. Making the presentation is board chairman H. Naylor Fitzhugh, a Pepsi Cola Company vice president

special markets vice president of Pepsi Cola Company.

A few years ago, a longtime friend, who still is a member of NAMD, James "Bud" Ward, told me that the organization in the latter part of the 1990s had changed its name to the National Alliance of Market Developers, Inc. In subsequent conversations with Charles "Chuck" Smith, who was a representative for Royal Crown Cola in the 1960s, and Allen MacKellar, who was with Falstaff Beer, I learned of the continuing activities of NAMD.

XIV

Doing More "Educating" at Humble Oil

My position with Humble Oil as National Community Relations Coordinator allowed me some very special privileges too. Whenever I went to the headquarters in Houston, I had the opportunity to meet personally with the president, Dr. Charles Jones. I had met Charles when he was president of Esso Research and Engineering Company, so, when he became Humble's president and we talked, he always asked me, "O.K. Jim tell me what are we doing wrong?" Since marketing management knew I could get to him personally, I was given unusual respect. I recall receiving a letter from black employees in a marketing district in Texas in 1965 where separate eating facilities and bathrooms were still in use. I visited that district and found that the segregated facilities did exist. I met with the employees and then the manager. I told him that I would give him two weeks to correct the problem or I would report it to higher authorities. He wasted no time in eliminating the segregated restroom and the segregated dining facilities for employees. When he wrote me about it, I sent him a letter commending him on his leadership. The black employees sent me a warm note of appreciation for making sure that those segregated facilities were removed.

Once, while conducting business in New Orleans, the Vice President of Public Relations called and asked me to come to the Houston headquarters as soon as possible. On arrival, I found that management was upset about a banquet black people were going to hold in the Humble building's main dining room, a banquet-sized dining room that was often used by community organizations. In the words of the vice president, "A communist was going to be the guest speaker." I soon found out that he was referring to Dr. Martin Luther King! To give him some idea of the significance of the dinner, I gave him a lengthy background of the attainments and prestige of Dr. King on behalf of equal justice and equal opportunity for all Americans. I also told him about the outstanding local black leaders who would be present, people such as Hobart Taylor Senior, an advisor to President Lyndon Johnson; John Chase, a prominent architect; and Dr. C. W. Thompson, a well-known physician. I gave him information on city councilmen, educators, and other civic leaders along with members of the white community who would be attending this important banquet given by the Twentieth Century Club of Houston. This situation was more evidence of the need for our top management to get more education on all aspects of race relations. Of course, it was my job to see that they did.

When we became part of Humble Oil in 1960, there was only one black in the entire headquarters building in Houston above the janitor role, and he was in the duplicating department. Some of the whites in top management had a hard time properly pronouncing the word Negro. It always sounded like "Negra" to me. I knew then that it would not be an easy task working with Humble's management advising them on race relations and getting them to make important employment moves. At that time, the words "diversity in the work place" were not in the corporate language. One of the things I had to do was to give them a better understanding of the importance of the black community in terms of the dollars spent on petroleum products. It was also important for them to know that our company had to practice equal employment opportunity at all of our locations, not just because it was the right thing to do, but because it presented the company as an enlightened marketer. There were no internal recruitment programs in the southern-based company or structured job-training endeavors geared to upgrade and promote minorities. I counseled our employee relations people on employment sources and on how to proceed with interviews. I also assisted our headquarters people in bringing in young capable blacks for interview opportunities for various clerical and sales positions. In later years, I often wondered if any of the black employees that worked there, a number of who had moved upward into higher job levels, realized the groundwork that had been laid for them.

I recall a letter I received in December 1961 from Carl Reistle, Jr., who was President of Humble at that time. In the letter he wrote:

> Dear Mr. Avery:
>
> I read with great interest your article, "Negroes in America...Changes in Attitude and Action," which was prepared for inclusion in the booklet given Mr. Ramsey (a Humble Board Member) during his recent visit to the Eastern Esso Region. May I commend you for the thought-provoking information you presented and for the outstanding effort you are making so that Humble can serve all the people in the United States in a way that will warrant their respect, confidence, and loyalty.

I knew there were many executives in the Humble Company who needed to have information so they could better understand the need for our company to be more aware of our marketing challenges and to be more progressive in our overall business practices. That objective was a continuing priority for me.

All during this time, I continued my community service activities in Plainfield, New Jersey. The March 1964 issue of the *Humble News* carried a story of my activities. The title of the story was "Others Thought I Could Lead" (which is where we got the title of this autobiography). The first paragraph was a quote from me. It stated:

"We are here to make use of ourselves. My Mother taught me that and what she said has been part of my life ever since. If I have an interest in my community—and every citizen should—then I want to help solve its problems."

"Such views, stated the article, " are part of the personal philosophy behind a lifetime of service for Jim Avery, a citizen of Plainfield, New Jersey, and public relations representative in the Eastern Esso Region Office."

XV

Working with the United Negro College Fund

I enjoyed my community activities and felt it was extremely meaningful to our company's public relations and marketing goals. A very interesting participation was my involvement with the United Negro College Fund (UNCF). When I joined the company in 1956, Esso, through its Esso Education Foundation, had been giving an annual grant to UNCF. During my involvement with this activity in the 1960s, that grant climbed from $50,000 to $150,000. Each year, along with a company vice president, Wendell Alston and I would make the presentation to the person who was the executive director of UNCF. The first of several presentations where I was involved were with Dr. Fred Patterson, a former Tuskegee University president, who along with Dr. Mary McLeod Bethune, had initiated the United Negro College Fund in 1944 with 27 member institutions. Following Dr. Patterson was Bill Trent who later ended up in a management role with *Time* Magazine. Dr. Steven Wright, former president of Fisk College,

Dr. Fred Patterson, former president of Tuskegee Institute and the original president of the United Negro College Fund, points out some college locations to Jim Avery, the Esso Standard Oil executive and national vice chairman of the 1966 annual fund-raising campaign, and Carl Anderson of Merck & Co., chairman of the campaign

and James Bryant, a former college administrator, were later executive directors when we gave our annual Esso Education Foundation grant of $150,000. After each presentation, our press people would send out a press release with photos to the members of the black press so the Esso Education Foundation grant received extremely wide publicity.

I was invited, in 1965, to become a national vice chairman for the United Negro College Fund working with Mike Heider, Chairman of the Esso Standard Oil Board and chairman of the 1965 campaign. In 1966, Carl Anderson, vice president of Merck, was national chairman, and again I was asked to be national vice chairman. I continued in 1967 as a national vice chairman when Dudley Dowell, a New York based corporate executive, was national chairman of that year's campaign. I enjoyed going around to various cities making speeches at fund raising campaign dinners. My visit to Buffalo to speak at their annual UNCF Report Dinner in October 1966 was one of the many occasions. The Buffalo *Evening News* reported:

Jim Avery, speaking at Buffalo Banquet. Looking on are J. Milton Zeckhouser, UNCF Bd. Chr. for the area, and Robert Land Miller, Chr. of Western NY State UNCF

> Never has the role of the United Negro College Fund's member colleges been more promising or more essential to the nation's welfare and security than now," James S. Avery of Humble Oil & Refining Company told the annual report dinner of UNCF in the Statler-Hilton Hotel. "For thousands of students, colleges like those supported by UNCF, will of necessity continue to be the major pathway to learning in the years ahead.
>
> Avery, who is Community Relations Coordinator for Humble, the largest U.S. oil refiner and marketer, is also national vice chairman of this year's United Negro College Fund campaign for $5,665,000. He was the main

speaker at the Buffalo dinner attended by 200 community leaders and campaign workers.

Articles of this kind appeared in the various cities when their annual United Negro College Fund meetings were held. In the many talks I gave, I focused on one major area, the need for preparedness on the part of all segments of our society. I stated:

> At no time in our country's history has the higher educational development of larger segments of non-white youth held more promise, and at the same time, been more essential to the nation's welfare and our future national security. Negro Americans are becoming an increasingly larger segment of our overall population of a growing number of our central cities. To mention a few: Chicago is 25% Negro, Philadelphia 26%, New Orleans 37%, St Louis 29%, Birmingham 41%, Atlanta 38%, Memphis 38%, Cleveland 30%, Detroit 29%, Washington D.C. 54%, Newark 50%, and Baltimore 40%.
>
> These population changes take on great significance when we realize that as the nonwhite population increases in our major cities, it will have a proportionately greater impact on the economic well-being of these strategic urban areas. Negroes will make up a greater share of the potential consumers, more of those who comprise the labor market, and a larger number of those who will guide the development of young people in the community.
>
> I think we all agree that our urban centers cannot be efficient producing and consuming units unless the great bulk of the population has the education and training for productive pursuits in jobs, avocations, and in family and civic life. In today's complex society, responsible citizenship, no matter what its form, requires a base of educational preparation that makes the acquisition of knowledge and skills a must for us all.
>
> The problem is not whether these schools are needed. That is not the problem or the question. It is whether Americans in sufficient numbers, Negro and

> white, businessman, philanthropist, citizen, are ready to recognize the seriousness of the need for greater effort in expanding the opportunities for higher education among Negroes and to improve the quality of that education as well.
>
> Most of our UNCF schools have served generations of students in their efforts toward self-discovery and in the struggle to make the American ideal real and meaningful. When no other resource was available, when the doors of the general society remained firmly and sometimes fiercely closed, when no form of power, political, economic, or moral, was at hand to wage the battle for equal opportunity, education via the predominantly Negro colleges was often the only road toward the promise of the future. So much has depended upon these colleges in the past, the development and survival of an entire people, and so much is now thrust upon their resources that the burden is awesome and almost overwhelming.

The manager of the Humble Oil Company's headquarters Public Relations Department sent copies of the talk I gave in Buffalo, on the significance of the United Negro College Fund, to all the major offices in the company. In his cover letter, he said:

> We believe you will be interested in J. S. Avery's recent address given at the annual report banquet of the Buffalo (N.Y.) United Negro College Fund. Among other significant points is the rationale made for continuing support for some years ahead of predominantly Negro colleges in the United States—a question which may be raised from continued support by the Company.

The population figures that I used in those talks in 1966 were taken from the U.S. Census reports. At the time, they were astonishing and made a real impact in the messages that I gave. I enjoyed my tenure as a national vice chairman for the United Negro College Fund and served in that capacity for annual campaigns from 1965 to 1967. I was especially proud of the fact that during the years I served in that capacity, we raised more than $12 million for UNCF colleges and universities. The Fund has been in existence for over 60 years and during that time has raised over $2 billion dollars and has served over 300,000 students.

One of the things I treasure most and still have in my possession is a compilation of thank you letters given me in December of 1965 by UNCF from the various college and university presidents involved in the Fund. A compilation of some of the statements made by the various presidents in these letters are as follows:

Dr. Rufus E. Clement, president of Atlanta University, said: "May I take this occasion to thank you, in the name of this great university, for the great help you have been to us all."

Dr. Lionel H. Newsom, president of Barber-Scotia College, said: "Words alone are much too inadequate to covey how important your contribution has been to keep our colleges moving forward to more higher standards and more adequate facilities....Our colleges in general and Barber-Scotia in particular, will long remember how you labored to make our survival possible and our future bright."

Dr. Willa B. Player, president of Bennett College, said: "Our faculty and students are deeply appreciative of your efforts in our behalf. They join me in expressing our gratitude to you for the personal interest which you have shown and for the accompanying hard work required by your acceptance of the responsibility to help."

Dr. Richard V. Moore, president of Bethune-Cookman, College said: "It is individuals like you who inspire us to continue our task of Christian education."

Dr. M. K. Curry, Jr. said: "The decision of the Directors of the Fund to seek a larger goal contributed greatly to the achievement of new dimensions of support. But, of greater significance was the acceptance on the part of community leaders like you to make this dream come true."

Dr. Vivian W. Henderson, president of Clark College, said: "We are grateful and deeply indebted to you as one of the persons whose interest and leadership helped to make the 1965 United Negro College Fund Campaign a successful one."

Dr. A. W. Dent, president of Dillard University, said: "Your dedicated effort in the interest of providing higher educational opportunities for Negroes as expressed through your service to the United Negro College Fund is sincerely and deeply appreciated by myself and all of my colleagues in Dillard University."

Dr. Steven J. Wright, president of Fisk University, said: "... our thoughts turn to the long, hard hours of work represented by the success of the campaign, and to you, one of our National Vice Chairmen, who gave unstintingly of your time, energy, and wisdom to make this campaign a success."

Dr. Jerome H. "Brud" Hollard, president of Hampton Institute, said: "It made me feel very good to see an old friend involved in such an important matter. We are all deeply indebted to you."

Dr. John Q. Taylor King, president of Huston-Tillotson College, said: "We are thoroughly cognizant of the fact that the colleges could not have progressed as they have without the dedicated services which you have rendered in your office."

Dr. Harry V. Richardson, president of The Interdenominational Center, said: "Please know that as a result of your efforts many a young person is getting a chance at a higher life which otherwise they would not have had."

Dr. R. P. Perry, president of Johnson C. Smith College, said: "As national vice chairman of the Fund's 1965 campaign, your contribution to the effort has been a heartwarming demonstration of your interest and faith in the value of the member colleges of the Fund in our national life."

Dr. James S. Colston, president of Knoxville College, said: "You efforts in our behalf make it possible for us to send out into the world many grateful young people who contribute to the welfare of our society."

Dr. C. A. Kirkendoll, president of Lane College, said: "The trustees, faculty, and students of Lane College join me in expressing appreciation to you for your fine leadership in the 1965 UNCF Campaign."

Dr. S. E. Duncan, president of Livingston College, said: "When we review the success of the 1965 UNCF Campaign we do so with great appreciation of the services you rendered as a leader in this most worthwhile venture."

Dr. Hollis F. Price, president of LeMoyne College, said: "The colleges could not get along without UNCF and the type of leadership you have given as National Vice Chairman."

Dr. Benjamin E. Mays, president of Morehouse College, said: "As one of the presidents of the member colleges I take this opportunity to express in an inadequate way my sincere thanks and appreciation for your leadership."

Dr. John A Middleton, president of Morris Brown College, said: "Because of your leadership in the campaign, we have reached a new high water mark in fund raising."

Dr. A. V. Pinkney, president of Oakwood College, said: "May the joys of your singular and collective achievement as National Vice Chairman be surpassed only by the accumulated enrichment which the Campaign has brought to many underprivileged young people."

Dr. E. Clayton Calhoun, president of Paine College, said: "To have given such significant leadership to the United Negro College Fund in a period of great advance must give you a sense of deep satisfaction. I assure you that it inspires our deepest gratitude."

Dr. Ernest T. Dixon, president of Philander Smith College, said: "You have my highest regards and sincere best wishes for continued success and happiness in your good work."

Dr. James A. Boyer, president of Saint Augustine's College, said: "Speaking for Saint Augustine's College, I am happy and proud to know that we still have such dedicated leadership as that represented by your service as a National Vice Chairman for this year's Drive."

Dr. Earl H. McClenney, president of Saint Paul's College, said: "Needless to say, the success of the campaign was due in large measure to your untiring efforts and outstanding leadership."

Dr. James E. Cheek, president of Shaw University, said: "We shall not soon forget the spirit of love for fellowman and deep dedication to education which your work has thus exemplified."

Dr. A. E. Manley, president of Spelman College, said: "Your work as National Vice Chairman during the 1965 Campaign was directly responsible for its success. We are sincerely grateful that you, who are so busy with your own and civic affairs should take time out to help us achieve our goal."

Dr. K. O. Broady, Acting President of Stillman College, said: "Your efforts in the national campaign not only realize funds for our institutions, but they are also evidences of your abiding interest in our work which is so significant in this period of our country's life and development."

Dr. Herman H. Long, president of Talladega College, said: "You have joined your interest with the cause of these colleges and of higher education, and for this there is no adequate response of gratitude we can give. But, I hope you feel rewarded in the knowledge that you have helped provide opportunity for an entire generation of young people. Without your assistance and that of men and woman like yourself, this bridge to the future would not have been built."

Dr. L. H. Foster, president of Tuskegee Institute, said: "We are especially appreciative of your splendid contributions to the success of our efforts, Mr. Avery. Your services as national Vice Chairman of the 1965 Campaign have been most helpful in assisting us to provide programs for the maximum development of the young people who are enrolled with us."

Dr. T. W. Cole, Sr., president of Wiley College, said: "The President and all members of the "Wiley College Family"—Trustees, Administrators, Faculty, staff members, students, alumni, church and local groups, and friends wish to express sincere appreciation to you for what your efforts have meant to the growth of Wiley College."

Sister M. Maria Stella, president of Xavier University of Louisiana, said: "It is fitting that a message of appreciation and gratitude be sent to you in recognition of your outstanding services to the United Negro College Fund of which organization Xavier has been a member since 1947."

This time in the 1960s was a critical period in the history and progress of UNCF colleges and universities. Each of these presidents must go down in the annals of American education as dynamic, committed leaders that brought these wonderful institutions safely through such trying times.

XVI

Plans for Progress

During the course of my various organizational meetings, I had become familiar with some of the business people in the Plans for Progress program. Plans for Progress was initiated by the Johnson Administration to encourage major corporations across America to put in place plans for increasing the training and the hiring of minorities, for utilizing the services of minority companies, and for putting real life into the recently enacted Civil Rights Act. In 1964, I had the special privilege of being selected with a group of Plans for Progress VIPs to be taken to Huntsville, Alabama, to the facilities of Cummings Engine Company to witness the construction of the Saturn Five rocket. Cummings Engine had the contract from the National Aeronautics and Space Administration to design and build this powerful mechanism. The precision involved in every aspect of its construction was simply overwhelming. Men were looking at seams with magnifying glasses to make sure there were no spots of weakness, others were sanding the sides as delicately as one would a precious stone. One had to get special clearance from Washington before being allowed anywhere near the NASA operations, and I felt very special to be so honored.

I had the same feeling in May 1972 when I was selected by the United States First Army Air Command based in Newburgh, New York, to go with a group of northeast U.S. VIPs to see some very special United States air defenses. We went to a number of strategic locations in America, including one near Los Alamos, New Mexico, where we saw the heat-seeking missile in action. After that we were flown to Camp Crowder in Colorado where we were taken into Cheyenne Mountain to see the Air Force Command Center located there. Amazingly, a virtual city with streets and buildings had been built within that mountain and there was sophisticated, computerized equipment that allowed the authorities to monitor the entire sky over the United States at any time, day or night. Very few people outside of government circles have been allowed into Cheyenne Mountain. What a privilege to be one American who can say that he has been on the inside!

When the Johnson Administration announced the Plans for Progress Program, they must have known it was not going to be an easy sell. After all, the word was coming from a Democratic administration known for its liberal stance. Some companies viewed the program as a government promotion, and they let their fear of "creeping federalism" affect their participation. Other companies with poor records in minority group employment felt signing a Plans for Progress agreement was merely a harmless reassertion of a long-standing policy of equal and fair hiring without regard to race, color, or creed. Far from being good public relations, instead of encouraging a favorable attitude toward business, the company whose records contradicted its statements inadvertently added fuel to the existing fire of distrust. The lure of government contracts, however, was an attractive incentive and many companies saw the wisdom of getting involved. Vice President Hubert Humphrey took leadership in another direction. He knew that to push for equal employment was one thing, but there had to be a corollary push to make sure there were prospective employees available when opportunities arose.

Jim Avery shaking hands and chatting with Vice President Hubert H. Humphrey

In January of 1965, I received an invitation from Vice President Hubert H. Humphrey to attend a meeting and discuss the development of a Task Force on Youth Motivation, to be coordinated under the auspices of the

Plans for Progress Program. I attended the meeting and agreed to be a member of the Advisory Committee to the Vice President's Task Force on Youth Motivation. In fact, I was selected to be its Vice Chairman. The main objectives of this Task Force were to visit predominantly black high schools and colleges to inform students about the new opportunities available to them in business and industry. It was felt this message would be more effective coming from blacks who had attained responsible positions in business and industry and were living witnesses. In April 1965, 65 black business executives met at the Decatur House to hear the purpose of the task force explained by Vice President Hubert H. Humphrey, Secretary of Labor, Willard Wirtz, and others from the Plans for Progress Advisory Council.

Business and industry representatives at a Plans for Progress meeting, 1965

In the Spring of 1965, 41 Task Force representatives visited 42 colleges and the response was overwhelming. Later that year, as a member of the Task Force Advisory Council, I participated in a meeting in Washington to outline the second phase of this program, which included visits to high schools, speeches before student assemblies, group meetings with student leaders, and discussions with school administrators and guidance personnel. In addition to visiting the colleges, we helped each college to organize an Advisory Campus Student Committee of Plans for Progress that could arrange for local Plans for Progress companies to consult with students on job demands, requirements, preparation of resumes, and the like.

I did not think enough was being done by business and industry to meet Plans for Progress goals. At the Plans for Progress Conference in Washington in January 1968, I felt a strong need to speak very candidly on the subject of equal employment opportunity. In my comments I said:

> I'm speaking today from the standpoint of a concerned businessman—not one who will attempt to justify existing inadequacies but one who is anxious to see greater commitment and action. I am one who believes that business and industry have made considerable progress in equal employment—moving from a posture of little or no involvement to one of increased enlightenment. However, the gap that exists between present socio-economic conditions and those we must reach before there is a level of real achievement is still far too wide. Many problems and obstacles still remain. Some, though by no means all, are due to natural independent methods of business operations; others are due to a lack of understanding of conditions and problems; still other problems relate to a failure to eliminate continuing forms of job discrimination. All of these factors individually, and in some cases collectively, have impeded the progress companies should be making in improving minority-group employment. These factors have also contributed to a lack of faith and belief that business is making a sincere effort. The results are reflected not only in attitudes in the minority-group community but in the attitudes of many less enlightened businessmen themselves. It is unfortunate that the inaction of the past years, when enlightened programs of employment were not fashionable, still colors the attitudes and reactions of both the white and black communities.

Throughout that conference we stressed the fact that more needs to be done by business and industry both in terms of communicating action programs and in terms of finding more and better ways to increase the percentage of minority-group employment.

In 1967, after serving as vice chairman of the Advisory Council to the Task Force, I was chosen to be its Chairman. I thoroughly enjoyed the experience of working with the Vice President of the United States on such an important matter. I sat on the dais with him and had many personal chats about the program. I especially liked his warm, congenial way of relating to people, even though he always did it in a formal way. "Mr. Avery," he once said, "I believe we have a formula here that will generate a great deal of success in encouraging minority youth to higher levels of aspiration. You know, that makes me very happy." I had the pleasure of meeting and chatting with his wife a number of times also. She was a very charming, lovely person who was certainly a great asset to him. My involvement with the Plans for Progress Program was most rewarding and my experience with the Vice President was unforgettable. I treasure the pictures taken with Vice President Humphrey and President Lyndon Johnson. These photographs document my extraordinary experience with the Plans for Progress Program.

Jim Avery shaking hands with President Lyndon B. Johnson in the White House Oval Office

XVII

Speaking Out

While I was Humble's National Community Relations Coordinator, I had the opportunity to make a number of very important speeches. Several of these speeches were published in pamphlet form and sent out by our Headquarters Public Affairs people in Houston to thousands of individuals and organizations and to various company locations around the country. One of the best and most significant speeches was the commencement address I gave in 1965 at Philander Smith College in Little Rock, Arkansas. It was entitled, "Our Responsibility for the Development of Human Talent." In my address to the graduating seniors I pointed out that:

Opportunities are now open on the broad job front in this country and you can make your own way as long as you bring competence and ability with you. Let us realize that new legal language and new laws of themselves do not assure new opportunities. Every opportunity implies an obligation. Ours is to prepare, to outfit ourselves with the cloak of education and training, just as you graduates have done. It isn't that we have a choice really whether to get it or not—we have no choice. Either we develop the skills and utilize our talents to the highest degree or we end up in a world of lost dreams and unfilled opportunities.

In the last part of my address I said these words with the utmost of sincerity:

> Today, (1965) 55% of the earth's population is under 25. In the United States, the average age of our citizens is dropping each year and by 1968, the average American will be 25 years old. An increasing number of these

young people will be Negro. In the New World of technology and changing human relationships, you can easily see why it is imperative that our young people be capable, intelligent, well educated, and well trained.

This is why each of you must use this education and employ your human talents to the great task ahead. IF YOU ARE TO TEACH—then be unsatisfied as long as there is one youngster in your class with hopes and aspirations unfulfilled. IF YOU ARE TO BE MEN OF GOD—then work unceasingly to stem the tide of growing immorality and in turn make Christian precepts a part of the every day life of all people. IF YOU ARE TO JOIN INDUSTRY—then search your qualifications and by your competence and your ability constantly improve your performance—motivating others by your example. IF YOU ARE TO FACE THE CHALLENGE OF SOCIAL WORK—then light the lamp of self-respect and dignity in the lives of the weak and unfortunate. As you organize groups and communities for self-help, the consumer becomes a producer as well, driving out many of the distorted images that blind us to racial and social reality. Whatever you do—use those human talents for the benefit of mankind. Whatever you do, pursue your goals with a fervent dedication, seek the excellence that is often reflected in the uncommon performance of average men who put forth that extra effort. Carry with you that sense of urgency and concern that drives away indifference—that recognizes and rejects all that is unworthy within us; that spirit which seeks to render things better—or, at least, better understood.

Jim Avery as guest speaker before the Baytown, Texas Human Relations Commission's Annual Dinner, 1967

Humble received hundreds of complimentary letters about this address from leaders in business, industry, and civic life. *Chemical Week* magazine featured it as a full-page article in its editorial column "Viewpoint" entitled, "A Beckoning Path and a Burden."

One of the other speeches made in 1967 at a banquet given by the Baytown, Texas, Community Relations Council and published by the company for wider circulation was called, "The Nation and the Neighborhood." That one was also extremely well received. In that speech I stressed that:

> The major challenges in human relations lie in areas that are outside and beyond the law. They deal, rather, with men's minds and hearts—with what one believes and feels, often with powerful and ingrained behavioral patterns.
>
> The unsolved problems of disadvantaged America—especially those of Negro Americans—have a direct bearing upon a multitude of other even broader social concerns. The struggle for full opportunity for this minority is, in the widest sense, the struggle of us all for the healthy growth of our cities and our society at large.

I pointed out that:

> Community acceptance and support of local community relations organizations depend upon the ability of such groups to deal with issues that are difficult, complex, and sometimes explosive. This means, in short, that success will largely depend on the degree and pace with which each specific project cuts to the heart of a community problem.
>
> Those who call for divisive positions are turning their back on ideals. We must not allow a few to embitter or disillusion the many with false logic, the kind that could deflect us from a course of fairness and justice.

The year 1967 was a pivotal one for me. Before the end of that year I had been promoted to a mainstream position, one of the most important in the company. I was promoted to Public Relations Manager for Humble's Northeastern Marketing Region Headquarters, the largest sales region in the United States! Our total sales in that region equaled the sales of the 115th company in the Fortune 500 listing! In that role I was responsible for overall corporate public relations in a region including New York, New Jersey, Massachusetts, Connecticut, Vermont, Maine, New Hampshire, and Rhode Island. I had a staff of seven people who assisted me in our media and community relations, in the counseling of management on local environmental issues and trends within this geographic area and in the development and implementation of programs designed to involve the company in positive ways in urban affairs. I was the first African American to ever hold such an important position in the oil industry.

Not long after being promoted to Public Relations Manager, I received a letter from a friend of mine, Harvey Russell, who was also in the National Association of Market Developers and was a Vice President for Pepsi Cola. Harvey, incidentally, was the first African American to be a vice president for any major American corporation. In his letter he asked if I would accept a position as Vice President of Special Markets for Pepsi Cola. I had met Mr. Barnett (I don't recall his first name) who was President of Pepsi Cola when I was active with the Plans For Progress Program and chairman of Vice President Humphrey's Task Force on Youth Motivation. The invitation to join Pepsi must have been endorsed by him. Anyway, I thought long and hard about it but ended up not accepting the offer. I felt that, on a long-term basis, I was better off staying with Esso Standard Oil Corporation which, after all, was the number one corporation in the Fortune 500 listing.

I told my management of the receipt of the letter from Harvey Russell and of my decision not to accept his offer. I responded to Harvey, thanking him for the opportunity he offered me, and suggested that he contact Dr. H. Naylor Fitshugh, head of Howard University's Marketing Department. Harvey must have taken my advice, for several months later it was announced that "Fitz" as we called him, resigned from his position at Howard University, accepted Harvey's offer and became an outstanding member of Pepsi's management team from 1969 until his retirement in the early 1980s.

While I was involved with the Plans for Progress program, Pepsi Cola's president was its chairman. Interestingly, he asked me if I would join that program as its executive director. Again, after consulting with Esso's management, I declined the offer. The position with the Plans for Progress program was accepted by my friend Gus Peterson, who worked for The Hartford Insurance Company. Following his experience with Plans for Progress, Peterson accepted a position in the Business Department of Stanford University. In later years, Peterson became the director of Hartford's new (at the time) sports arena.

While I was Public Relations Manager of Esso's Northeastern Region, I was asked to represent a member of the Board of Directors of Standard Oil of New Jersey on the Committee for Economic Development (CED). The group was to do a study concerning the education of minorities who were educationally and economically disadvantaged. Located in New York City, CED was a highly regarded "think tank" that studied critical issues in education and, through meetings and seminars with experts, developed a position paper that was publicized through the appropriate educational channels. These reports were circulated throughout the nation to public and private leaders in educational matters laying the seedbed for important action on the subject. I believe I was asked to take part because Esso's management knew of my previous involvement in both secondary and higher educational levels. I reported back to the corporation on my participation. CED published a paper on the subject that put an important spotlight on this critically important and emerging issue. While I have no solid proof of it, the Educational Opportunity Fund program that Governor Thomas Kean of New Jersey started in 1968, in which I later became involved, could have been a follow-up of the activities of the Committee for Economic Development.

XVIII

The Union County New Jersey Project

While still the Public Relations Manager for Esso, I was continually encouraged to participate in civic affairs. Consequently, in 1968, I was appointed by the Board of Chosen Freeholders of Union County to serve on a newly enacted agency named the Union County Coordinating Agency for Higher Education for a term of four years. This agency was responsible for utilizing Union College with campuses in Cranford, Elizabeth, and Plainfield along with the Union County Technical Institute in Scotch Plains to provide a system of comprehensive community college services for Union County. This agency was created by legislation passed in 1966 that allowed any county in the state that did not have a public community college to create one through an existing private two-year college and an existing technical institute to provide a system of comprehensive community college services. At that time, Union County was the only county in the state that did not have a public community college. The purpose of the Coordinating Agency was not to operate a community college but to coordinate existing operations, support it financially, oversee it, support its efficiency, and develop its services so that they would be truly comprehensive.

Union County College was founded in 1933 as Union County Junior College, a federally sponsored public institution. It began classes at night at Abraham Clark High School in Roselle, New Jersey. Sometime in the early 1940s, the college moved to a building in Cranford on Eastman Street that had been a grammar school. My father, John Avery, had been a janitor at Union County Junior College in the 1940s and if he was still living he would have been so proud to know that 25 years later I became the chairman of the agency that was responsible for the educational system in which the former Union County Junior College was a key institution.

Two-year community colleges were becoming popular and a report of the Carnegie Commission on Higher Education predicted that the nation would need 300 new institutions of higher education by the year 2000, two thirds of them two-year community colleges.

In our first meeting, we called on the New Jersey State Department of Higher Education to provide $987,000 in state aid in the 1969–1970 academic year to help meet the higher education needs of the county. We also called on Union College to reduce its tuition to students of Union County to the same level charged by other county colleges in the state. We also asked the college to take the appropriate action with the State and the Middle States Association of Colleges and Secondary Schools to obtain the right to confer "Associate Degrees upon the graduates of the Union County Technical Institute who successfully completed college level programs acceptable to Union College." The Agency received and approved the annual budgets of the contracting institutions and reported actions taken to County Freeholders and the State Board of Higher Education. The Agency administered the state and county allocations and in accordance with contractual agreements reimbursed the institutions for services rendered.

There was tremendous benefit from this arrangement. A major one was the dramatic increase in the number of full-time students, and the diversity and the achievement level of the entering freshmen. Numerous programs were developed for the non-traditional student, such as the economically and educationally disadvantaged, the senior citizens, veterans, and the Spanish speaking. Affordability was another real benefit. New courses in such areas as nursing education, environmental engineering, and studies were added. The cooperating arrangement helped to double the number of courses and increase the non-credit program especially in the area of continuing education and remedial training.

The Daily Journal

TUESDAY EVENING, NOVEMBER 2, 1971 ★ THIRTEEN

News Of Western Union County

JAMES S. AVERY

Higher Education Group Renames Avery Leader

The Agency also worked on assuring the recruitment of minority students, evaluating procedures, implementing a single registration system for all programs, and revising the college handbook. Additionally, we completed a master plan that provided 20 new programs and nine administrative changes, consolidated computer operations, and developed a common database and master file. We did a great deal of work in the early years of the agency to build a solid higher education system in the county.

What we had in Union County, New Jersey, was a "county college" without major capital expenditures in educational plant facilities and faculty and staff recruitment and full accreditation from the beginning. These accomplishments would not have been possible without the existence of the Coordinating Agency for Higher Education. How proud I was to be chairman of this educational experience from its beginning for 12 consecutive years.

I was the guest of honor and the commencement speaker at the Union College Commencement in June of 1970. Each year thereafter, until I had to resign in 1980 I gave greetings at the commencement on behalf of the Agency. In my commencement address in 1970 I focused upon challenging the students to become more involved and concerned at the local level in

Grads Must Make Institutions "Relevant to the community"

CRANFORD--Union College graduates last week were urged to get involved in community activities "in order to tackle successfully the problems which surround us and constrict us" at the 37th annual commencement exercises.

The message came from James S. Avery of Scotch Plains, chairman of the Union County Coordinating Agency for Higher Education and Public Relations Manager of the Northeastern Region of Humble Oil and Refining Company.

"I would like to see each one of you accept a personal responsibility for doing what you can to help create the kind of environment in which new ideas, new attitudes and ways of doing things can emerge and develop," Mr. Avery said.

"Young people of America have the muscle, the brain and the heart power to remake the world. Historically, youth has always manifested a willingness to sacrifice everything when the purpose is big enough -- to put their lives on the line for great causes that inspire their faith

"GET INVOLVED"--Said Guest of Honor James S. Avery of Scotch Plains to the 144 Union College graduates at the 37th annual commencement exercises.

order to tackle successfully the problems that surround and constrict us. In my remarks to the graduates, I said:

> We need to move a significant share of the thrust of American life back to the individual in his local environment, back where he lives, where he does business, where he practices his chosen profession, where he teaches, and where he participates in government. This is a responsibility that must be placed in your hands, for we are talking about your world, your future, your investment in life here on earth. The only way to return substantial prerogatives and initiatives in community service, indeed in community life in general, is to foster the kind of environment that nurtures interest, participation and the involvement of all segments of the community. We are going to need a wide variety of effort on the local level, efforts that touch a diversified range of interest, some to devise new techniques of human relationships in educa-

tional and civic affairs altering or eliminating those that have been stifling to the human spirit.

Young people of America have the muscle, the brain, and the heart power to remake the world. Historically, youth has always manifested a willingness to sacrifice everything when the purpose is big enough. We need this sort of courage and energy to go to work on the fresh new approaches that must be found in order to tackle successfully the problems which surround us and constrict us.

I would like to see each one of you accept a personal responsibility for doing what you can to help create the kind of environment in which new ideas, new attitudes, and ways of doing things can emerge and develop. It would be up to you to make sure that our institutions and social processes are relevant to the lives of every segment of the community.

Relevancy should mean that everyone should be given power over his or her own life. We must plan with people not for people. Self-determination and the creation of a climate that allows the capacity for people to develop are absolute musts if we are to assure a relevant existence for people in America.

And, so it is in these times as our country turns full face in the task of human and physical rehabilitation and to the mammoth problems of coping with our technological environment. These of course are nationwide problems, but nowhere are the opportunities for improvement and benefit more prevalent, nowhere are the opportunities to achieve positive results better than within the towns an cities of Union County.

I was also privileged to give the commencement address at Union County Technical Institute's graduation ceremonies in June of 1973. In that address I talked about the need for human compassion. In it I said:

Let us remember that the world is so geographically shrunken and humanly expanded that man is indeed

> the brother of man. And whether we like it or not, regardless of ethnic group or class, each needs the other and is needed by the other. Since this is true, you have a responsibility as one who has some talent and ability to offer not to think only of your own goals, but of the impact that your presence can make in the world around you. You must develop a strategy for dealing with the dynamics of the power within you and join in the journey of making your community and your state a better and more wonderful place to live.

In 1980, Exxon moved its regional headquarters from Pelham, New York, to Norwalk, Connecticut, and I had to resign my chairmanship of the Union County Coordinating Agency for Higher Education. By then, despite the continuing resistance from the board of the Union County Technical Institute, we were coming close to completing the full development of what was to become Union County College. In my letter of resignation in December of 1980, I said:

> One does not easily sign off from a relationship of more than a decade with one of the most challenging and responsible of public service assignments. In the past 12 years, the Agency has labored long and hard to carry forth the mission to build a highly efficient community college system for the citizens of Union County. From its inception in 1969 as the first of its kind in the nation, its rewards, both fiscal and educational, have been and continue to remain boundless.
>
> I am saddened, as I leave, to think that there are still factions of the system that have not come to terms with the basic overriding priority, which is to fulfill their assigned roles for the achievement of an efficient, effective, cost-saving, high quality educational system. I am further saddened that for the first time since the inception of the Agency, these same factions have sought to politicize various issues at the expense of our higher education system. This is clearly detrimental to our students and other citizens of this county and to the

Agency, which is charged with the stewardship of the Community College in this county.

In my letter, I paid tribute to Dr. Kenneth C. McKay and Richard V. Lucas, the two directors of the Agency that served during my tenure. I paid tribute to a host of sincere and dedicated citizens who have served as members of the Coordinating Agency, the Boards, presidents, faculty and staff of Union College and Union County Technical Institute. I also acknowledged the fine working relationship with the Department of Higher Education and the broad-based and bi-partisan support of the Union County Board of Chosen Freeholders.

In the letter I could not ignore criticizing the members of the board of the Union County Technical Institute (UCTI). We could not understand why the board members felt they were equal to the college level board at Union College or why they continually made efforts to delay progress dealing with board status, degree granting, and other related matters.

When I submitted my resignation from the Union County Agency for Higher Education, I received a number of communications about it. Two letters from Union College are worth mentioning here. One of them was from the Dean of Student Affairs. In it he wrote:

> Dear Jim:
>
> As imminent as your departure may have been after your inferences at the Agency meeting earlier this fall, somehow I was not prepared for the reality of Dr. Orkin's correspondence confirming your departure from the Agency board. Obviously you could not continue your chairmanship of the Board indefinitely, yet I simply have grave difficulty considering the Board as an effective unit without your oversight.
>
> No statement that I can make will sufficiently express our loss by your departure. You were the single ingredient that provided the much needed cohesiveness and direction for the Board. The system will undoubtedly suffer a setback without you at the helm. However,

> let me join the many who wish you well in whatever manner of activity you intend to devote your time and talents to in place of Board service. I have personally benefited from observing your style and shall always treasure your acquaintance. Thank you for persisting in an attempt to insure quality education at the post-secondary institutions in Union County.
>
> Cordially,
> J. Harrison Morson
> Dean of Students, Union County College

The other was the letter I received in December 1980 from Dr. Saul Orkin, then president of Union College. In the letter, he said:

> I write to express the regret of the Union College Board of Trustees upon reading of your resignation from the Union County Coordinating Agency for Higher Education. Although we had had some forewarning of your imminent departure, the reality of it leaves us saddened.
>
> Certainly you have symbolized in your actions and statements over the years the usefulness of the Coordinating Agency to higher education in this county. Whatever contributions the Agency has made to the citizens of Union—I think they have been considerable—can be attributed directly to you. Your dedication, your leadership, your deep understanding of the educational system established here have made what began as an innovative idea into a functioning productive vehicle for delivering community college services where none had existed before. All of us in the County are indebted to you for what you have accomplished since the inception of the Agency in 1968. Union College appreciated your support and counsel through the years. During the time of your chairmanship of the Agency, this institution has experienced its greatest growth. It became more community serving and more comprehensive and I know it was not merely coincidence that our devel-

opment occurred during your tenure on the Agency Board.

Finally, I wish to express my warm personal thanks for your professional assistance and friendship. It has been a rewarding relationship that I hope will not end now.

The Board, faculty, and staff extend their best wishes to you as you take up residence in Connecticut. We expect you to visit us occasionally when you return to New Jersey.

Sincerely yours,
Saul Orkin
President, Union College

I am extremely proud of my involvement with the Union County Coordinating Agency for Higher Education and Union County College. Today, Union County Community College is one of the best and largest community colleges in the state and the only one with four campuses throughout Union County, New Jersey.

XIX

Moving Up in Omega's Leadership

As one with a very responsible position in the oil industry, very involved in several phases of community affairs, and at the time the Grand Basileus, national president of the Omega Psi Phi Fraternity, Inc., I was invited to address various groups on a number of occasions. I gave speeches for affairs held by Omega Psi Phi Fraternity chapters in selected cities in the United States. One of the most outstanding programs was held in El Paso, Texas. The Sigma Tau Chapter of the El Paso, Texas, and Las Cruses, New Mexico, area, invited me to be the keynote speaker for the 1971 annual Negro History Week program coordinated and sponsored by the Inter-Clubs Council of that same area. "Check My Credentials" was the theme of that week's celebration, and I made it the title of my speech. The El Paso *Herald Post* in reporting on my participation in an article on February 8, 1971 said:

Oil Company Executive To Keynote Negro Week

> The fabric of American life would be much different than it is without the contributions of the American Negro," James S. Avery, keynote speaker for Negro History Week, told an audience yesterday at Liberty Hall. Mr. Avery, public relations manager for the Northeastern Region of Humble Oil and Refining Company, spoke at a meeting sponsored by the Inter-Club Council of

> El Paso and Las Cruses. Tracing some of the accomplishments of many of the Negro scientists, educators, and statesmen, Mr. Avery said that much more can be accomplished by people working together, forgetful of prejudices and acknowledging true brotherhood.
>
> There is a gap between promises made to Negroes and the performances of those promises, he said. And those who argue that the arena of national society is too large should remind themselves that there is no one but themselves as individuals to work at the task of closing the gap. Confrontation is passe, he said, and what is required is that the Negro, as an individual, should be given the chance to present his credentials as a human being and as a qualified workman for whatever job he seeks.

It was an excellent week of activities in which other national level speakers participated, among them my friend and fraternity brother, the Reverend Jesse Jackson, who spoke on Wednesday evening of that week.

The courtesies extended to me by members of Sigma Tau Chapter were fabulous. Our participation in a radio show on black history received wide mention and the receptions with business and civic leaders of the community were extremely well attended. Special kudos went to brothers like Willie Brather, Wilmer Gray, Jefferson Jenkins, Samuel Smoak, and Jethro Hills, all members of Sigma Tau Chapter.

Four members of the Sigma Tau chapter of the El Paso, Texas-Las Cruses, New Mexico area welcomes Brother Grand Basileus, February, 1971, as the keynote speaker for the chapter's weeklong Negro History celebration

Despite having a number of major responsibilities in business and civic life, I was still very active in my fraternity. During the early part of the sixties, I moved up the ranks of the fraternity's district in which I lived, which happens to be called the Second District, from being the Director of Public Relations, to being the First Vice District Representative, and finally to becoming the head of the district, the Second District Representative. I also participated as a national traveling representative for the fraternity. In this role it was my responsibility at our grand conclaves to report my observations and suggestions for improvement in policy and programs that came to mind as a result of my traveling around the country and visiting with the brothers and chapters.

At the national conclave in Detroit, Michigan, in 1965, I pointed out:

> In a number of cities, I have met brothers who could not claim association with any chapter—many who were not financial nationally. In other cities there were chapters moving listlessly along on the power of periodic social affairs—seemingly oblivious to many of the real needs and challenges in the community. Chapter meetings were being held where more emphasis was placed on the activities that occurred after the meeting rather than on the business of the meetings themselves. This does not leave a good picture when fraternities are under increasing criticism. It is not encouraging when one of our most serious concerns is the loss of active participation of brothers. It is downright appalling at a time when we must find ways to make every brother—undergraduate and graduate alike—so imbued with the philosophy of Omega, so desirous of preserving Omega's ideals, that his discipline and his motivation propels him into constructive service in the chapter where he resides. Yes, wherever I went, I was sharply reminded that this matter of quality in our brotherhood is our greatest need.

The role of District Representative for one of the largest and most influential districts in the fraternity and as that of a national traveling representative gave me extremely high visibility in the fraternity. These positions gave me the opportunity to display my talents for analysis and evaluation, for public speaking and project development. As a District Representative, I developed an aggressive outreach program dealing with youth education and social issues and created a special think-tank activity called the Shirtsleeve Conference. This Brookings type of activity was a great success for it exemplified the kind of demeanor, attitude, commitment, and spirit that I wanted in Omega men. I created the Shirtsleeve Conference in 1965 and it has now been made a permanent part of the Second District's Constitution and By-laws and is held every fall. In later years, the national body in former Grand Basileus Moses Norman's administration adopted the Shirtsleeve idea for a national program that is now the fraternity's Bi-annual Leadership Conference.

During my administration as District Representative, we were adding chapters, principally graduate ones, in the Second District. As a result, it became difficult for me to participate in the activities of all the chapters because of scheduling conflicts. I chose to make some special appointments of brothers who could represent me at the various chapter functions. The first brother that I appointed to corridor representative was Rudolph W. Powell, an outstanding Omega man then living in New York. This procedure proved to be a very effective one for the Second District and was adopted in various ways by other districts within the fraternity.

As a district leader in the fraternity, I took every opportunity to speak out about the need for re-evaluation and reassessment of our values and our goals. One example was an article I wrote for the district's house organ, the *OMEGAN*, in 1967:

> A renaissance in thought and action is on the horizon and is about to manifest itself in the life of Omega. In one instance after another, the men of Omega are questioning the wisdom of perpetuating practices that are opposed to the Cardinal Principles of the fraternity. Many brothers are voicing strong concern for constructive social-action programming and vigorous progressive leadership. A growing percentage of brothers are indicating disenchantment with those who cling to outdated methods and to the idea that trivia and indignities have some place in Omega. An increasing number of Omega men want more programs and activities that

benefit the community and contribute to the solution of its problems. Let us not forget, no organization or institution can stand still, or live by or in its past. As I see it, more of us must join the movement to identify with the changes taking place, recognize our weaknesses and move to make adaptations necessary to insure that Omega will go first class in the future. This renaissance will grow and gain momentum for Omega men are recognizing that we have inherited a precious ideal, a special kind of brotherhood, formed into an organization for the service of mankind. For these reasons and by virtue of our compact we have an obligation to involve ourselves in the proper future development of Omega.

At various district conferences when I was District Representative, I made every effort to speak to high standards for the fraternity. At the conference in Buffalo, New York, in 1963, I told the brothers:

Socrates once said, "The unexamined life is one not worthy of being lived by one who calls himself a man." We call ourselves men, Omega men. If we love Omega as we say we do, it behooves us, therefore, to periodically examine our direction, to make sure that that we are following the pathway charted for us.

In speaking to the undergraduates at this conference, I said:

It is good to see our undergraduate brothers represented with us today. They have a great responsibility and a great opportunity to lead the way to a better image and a more secure future for Omega. Those of us who have been off the college campuses for more years than we care to remember may not realize that undergraduate chapters are under intense scrutiny and evaluation by college administrations. These chapters have an obligation to contribute positively to high academic standards, to manifest good social behavior and conduct constructive extracurricular activities, to contribute to the development of the intellectual life on the campus, and to cease being busy with trivia.

I was truly thrilled last month [March 1964] to witness our brothers at Beta Chapter at Lincoln University in Pennsylvania conduct a cultural program featuring Brother Langston Hughes, a world famous poet. The entire college community was present and one of the persons highest in his praise of the chapter was the president of Lincoln University, Dr. Wachman. Not only will such efforts engender the respect of faculty and administration, it cannot help but draw the caliber of man who seeks union with others of high aspiration who see the opportunities, the problems and responsibilities which are ours.

Langston Hughes, who died on May 17, 1967, was one of the best-known poets of his time and has gone down in history as one of the greatest. Through his works he kept alive the thoughts of a brighter future for the country and for better race relations. He encouraged all people to dedicate themselves to the betterment of society in which all racial groups must learn to live together. Langston used his poetic genius to chronicle and illuminate the black man's experience in America. How proud we were to have him as a member of our fraternity.

Second District Conference in Plainfield, NJ, 1964, hosted by Omicron Chi Chapter: from left, Brother Avery when he was district representative, Mayor Robert Maddox of the City of Plainfield, shaking hands with Brother Lovell Sutherland, Chapter Basileus and the Supreme Council's representative, editor to the oracle, Brother Aubrey Pruitt

At the district conference we held in Plainfield, New Jersey, in 1965, I appointed the district's first Social Action Chairman and its first Reclamation Chairman. Reclamation was a national theme that year. It was at this conference that I first announced the convening of a weekend Shirtsleeve Conference, where we would strive to get down to the bedrock of Omega. I wanted us to come out with a new vitality and a new perspective, bringing our objectives more in line with current needs and opportunities. At this district conference we also agreed to a project called "Operation Books" where we would amass thousands of books that we could send to Ondo, Western Nigeria, where Brother E. W. Waters, a former District Representative, was supervising a teacher training program. Most of the schools there were woefully inadequate in facilities, equipment, materials, and books. Brother Waters told us that books in science, history, literature, in fact, in all subjects were badly needed in the schools there. That year at the Shirtsleeve Conference we refined the project and under the leadership of Brother Lovell Sutherland, a member of Omicron Chi, our Second District chapters collected and sent many boxes of books to Western Africa to help young African students. Projects of this sort, the kind that made a real difference in the lives of others, was the kind of programming that I was advocating for us to carry out in Omega.

Brother Avery as Second District Representative presents a plaque of appreciation to Dr. E. W. Waters for his accomplishments as Past DR

At Omega's Grand Conclave in Detroit in 1965, a group of progressive minded young brothers led by Brothers Norman Johnson, Lloyd Bell, Ted Greer, and Milton Johnson came to me to encourage me to run for the office of First Vice Grand Basileus (like a national vice president). The idea was to position myself to eventually become Grand Basileus of the national organization. They expressed their disenchantment with the ole buddy system that was then prevalent at the national level and expressed total agreement with my ideas of moving the fraternity more aggressively in the area of social action. I agreed with the idea, and we developed an election strategy that resulted in my being elected two years later to the office of First Vice Grand Basileus of the Omega Psi Phi Fraternity, Inc.

It was in the summer of 1967 in Boston, Massachusetts, when I was sworn into office as First Vice Grand Basileus. I don't even remember if it was a contested election. The young brothers who made up my advisory team did a great job with placards and various other visual aids along with their personal contacts. I visited the various district caucuses too, telling them the commitment and programmatic plans I intended to bring to the office and to the fraternity. Brother Ellis Corbett, a publicist from Greensboro, North Carolina, who was on the staff of North Carolina A&T University, was our Grand Basileus at that time. He was a jovial, pleasant man who had been Editor of the *ORACLE*, our fraternity's house organ, prior to his move upward to Grand Basileus. We worked well together, and I spent the two years as his backup, evaluating programs, counseling on fiscal matters, and overseeing the work of the various committees.

Brother Ellis F. Corbett, Past Grand Basileus, congratulates Brother Jim Avery

I was elected Grand Basileus at the Grand Conclave in Pittsburgh, Pennsylvania, in 1970. My First Vice Grand Basileus was Brother Marion W. Garnett, who was a Chicago municipal judge. My Second Vice Grand Basileus was Brother Richard L. Taylor, an undergraduate Boston College student who became a Rhodes Scholar. The Grand Keeper of Records and Seal was Brother Charles D. Henry, a staff member at Grambling College in Louisiana. He later accepted a fine position with the NCAA. The Keeper of Finance was Brother John Moore from Charlotte, North Carolina. The Grand Counselor was Brother J. Franklin Spruil, an attorney from Indianapolis, Indiana. My choice as

Grand Chaplain was Father H. Albion Farrell, an outstanding Episcopalian cleric who had served all of our previous Grand Basilei since 1945. During the years when I was moving up the ranks of leadership in Omega and had the opportunity to hear Father Farrell speak, I was always impressed by his Christian logic, his dignity, and his eloquence. I was honored to have him serve as my Grand Chaplain.

One of the first things I did when I became Grand Basileus was to reorganize the Supreme Council, the ruling body of the fraternity, and put in place a system of accountability. I placed several committees under the leadership of Brother Garnett, committees such as Fraternity Programs, Personnel Administration, Community Housing, and Communications. Other committees were placed under the leadership of Brother Richard Taylor, committees such as Initiation and Procedures, Budget and Finance, Social Welfare, and Awards and Honors.

Those I appointed to chair the various national committees were all handpicked men, not chosen with any political concern but with the intent to pick those I felt were most able and most dedicated. Before appointing them I visited with each one to explain the objectives of my administration and to let them know what was expected of them. I selected Brother Otto McClarin to be Editor to the *ORACLE*, our fraternity's quarterly magazine. His background in journalism made him an excellent choice. I took a great deal of time to explain to him my concept of an *ORACLE* publication that was an intelligent, perceptive magazine that focused on major issues of interest and concern to the men of Omega. Brother Dr. Matthew Whitehead, a professor at District of Columbia College in Washington, D.C. , had been an outstanding and articulate chairman of our National Achievement Week Committee. When he found it impossible to continue, I appointed another outstanding educator, Dr. William A. McMillan, president of Rust College in Holly Spring, Mississippi. Brother McMillan brought a special dignity and significance to our national achievement activities. I continued Brother Wendell Morgan, an excellent fiscal mind, as our Budget Committee Chair. Brother Samuel Johnson was selected to chair the Undergraduate/Intermediate Chapters Committee. Brother Mark Hyman, an expert in the field of communications, served as my Director of Public Relations. Through his efforts we were continually mentioned in the black media highlighting our programmatic activities and our grand conclaves. Brother Moses C. Norman, a rising star in Omega at the time and an educational administrator in Atlanta, served as Chairman of our Reclamation Committee. I wanted the subject of scholarship, one of our cardinal principles, to be one of the priority issues of my administration. So I chose a terrific educator Brother Dr. Walter Ridley, then President of Elizabeth City College, to spearhead our National Scholarship Commission. Brother Riley was an aggressive and effective chairman who expanded the scholarships given out under the auspices of the commission. Brother Ridley was also responsible for coordinating my youth educational motivation program, called Project Aspiration, explained later in this chapter.

I had co-chairs for our Social Action Committee. One was Brother Dr. Lloyd Bell, an Assistant Provost at the University of Pittsburgh, and the other was Brother Samuel Chick Coleman of Newburgh, New York, whose specialty was in communications. Brother Bell was a respected civil rights activist who placed extra-special efforts on two of the initiatives of my administration, drug education and community health. Attorney Brother Jeff Greenup, a former Grand Counselor of our fraternity and a leading civil rights lawyer, served as chairman of our National Housing Authority. Brother Alphonso Patterson, an outstanding music teacher from Westchester County, New York, served as a fine chairman of our Talent Hunt Committee.

Brother Grand poses with Brother Jeff L. Greenup, former Omega Grand Counselor who served in Brother Avery's administration in 1970–73 as chairman of the fraternity's National Housing Authority

There were several important national issues highlighted during my administration. Increasing drug use was beginning to surface as a major national problem. The civil rights gains of the late 1960s were beginning to broaden economic opportunity for minorities. This focused a real need for improvement in personal health, educational development, and job preparedness. Problems of poverty were also getting heightened exposure as an issue of major national concern.

I had made it eminently clear when I became Grand Basileus of Omega Psi Phi Fraternity, Inc. that, in my view, Omega was not doing enough to make effective use of our talents in helping to ameliorate and solve some of the civic and social concerns of our communities. After all, we were part of the educated black population; why shouldn't we be the leaders in getting involved and utilizing our skills and abilities to help others in our communities? Social action projects were being carried out spottily on the local level but they were not unified national ones. I wanted to focus our national strength upon some areas where we could make a visible impact. That is why I initiated Project Uplift, a national drug education program in which all of our chapters could participate at the same time. We distributed thousands of bumper stickers to our chapters that read: "Omega says Stamp Out Dope." These bumper stickers were on automobiles and in store windows all across America. We gave out booklets, speech data and little handouts that helped parents, guardians, and others to identify the symptoms of drug use. Coordinated by our National Social Action Committee, it proved to be an excellent project that identified Omega with fighting a critically important national issue.

In 1972, I initiated Project Aspiration, a program geared toward motivating youth, particularly black youth, to higher educational attainment. Chapters were given the project design along with a certificate model and were asked to meet with school officials and parent groups and work out procedures for Omega's involvement in recognizing educational achievement by young boys. Project Aspiration was conducted under our Charles Drew Scholarship Commission. Many chapters are still conducting this project, but not with any organized support from our national leadership. Now, more than 30 years after my term as Grand Basileus, there remains a vital need to focus attention on the education of black youth.

In order to focus attention upon the health problems of blacks, we conducted a pilot Health O'Rama project. It was a realistic approach to combat inadequate information in such areas as mental and dental health, drug use, VD, pollution, and nutrition. Blood pressure testing was also available. The project was conducted in Nashville, Tennessee, in cooperation with Meharry Medical College and under the direct leadership of Brother Dr. Henry Moses. It was a success and represented a first in terms of a national fraternal organization joining with a medical center on such a large-scale community education project. It was carried out in 1973, and we strongly recommended its continuance in the administration that followed mine, but nothing was done to make it a national program. It was not until later in the 1990s, that the fraternity started to focus on health concerns at our Leadership Conferences.

During my administration as Grand Basileus, I made the *ORACLE* a clear manifestation of our new thrust of involvement and concern as well as our interest and identification with cultural matters. It was important to demonstrate what Omega men were doing in thought and deed to help solve the problems of our social environment as well as their impact upon the issues of race, racism, and human freedom at home and abroad. I wanted a publication that did not display the mundane social activities of our chapters but was a literary piece that featured major national issues and could be proudly displayed in libraries or professional offices around the country.

The fraternity's Life Membership Program was the brainchild of our National Executive Secretary Emeritus, the late Judge H. Carl Moultrie. It was voted into law by the Grand Conclave of 1958 in Cleveland, Ohio. Past Grand Basileus, Brother Cary D. Jacobs (1961-1964), was Life Member number one. Judge H. Carl Moultrie was Life Member number two. The program in those early days had accomplished little. For some unstated reason, there was the fear that such a program would destroy the local chapters and as a result, the activities relating to life membership lay virtually dormant. I revived the program at the 54th Grand Conclave in Houston in 1971 when I appointed Brother Walter "Crow" Riddick, Grand Keeper of Records and Seal Emeritus, as chairman of the Life Membership Program. I gave him the very challenging task of reviving it and creating an endowment for Omega. The total paid and partially paid life members at that time numbered only 47. The original goal was set at 1,000 members. Brother Riddick vowed to reach that goal during his tenure as Life Membership Chairman. The magic number of 1,000 was reached about the time that Brother Riddick entered Omega Chapter, July 23, 1977. Out of respect for his inspirational leadership and outstanding success, the 58th Grand Conclave mandated that Life Membership Number 1,000 be retired as a personal memorial to Chairman Emeritus Walter Crow Riddick.

Years later, in 1993, at a meeting of the Omega Life Membership Foundation (OLMF), I was elected to membership on the board and appointed to the executive committee. I served on the Foundation Board for the next seven years as the Investment Committee Chairman. It was my responsibility to develop strategies and guidelines and, through a structured investment decision-making process, take investment actions, which would produce the maximum total return on investments. Working closely with Brother Charles Peters, the comptroller, and Brother Harry Ratliff, our investment broker, this program helped the OLMF mutual fund investments increase 22%; corporate bond holdings increase 18%; and the fair market value of CD by 5%. I was very proud of the fact that the total corpus grew to over $2 million dollars during that period of the 1990s, while we continued to fulfill the organization's charitable objectives. I went off the OLMF board in 1999. I was delighted that Brother George K. McKinney, a retired United States Marshal for the state of Maryland, and later Brother Henry W. Glapsie would be coming into leadership roles bringing greater stability and continuing success to OLMF operations.

The Omega National Housing Development Corporation was set up in 1972 as an adjunct to the fraternity's National Housing Authority to stimulate action in the area of public housing. Brother Jeff Greenup as chairman had the specific challenge of linking Omega with the provision of public housing for the elderly. The Lambda Rho Apartments in Waterbury, Connecticut, was an outstanding example of Omega's involvement in this area. Completed in 1973, it was the first project for the minority elderly of its kind in the nation. At that time, other housing developments were in the planning stages by chapters in Washington, D.C., Miami, Florida, and Flint, Michigan. During his time as chairman of the Omega National Housing Authority, Brother Greenup initiated an original project called the "52-1 Plan." The object of the plan was to have each financial brother in the fraternity pledge one dollar a week for 52 weeks in the year to set up a "seed money fund" that local chapters could draw from to help them get chapter housing. Unfortunately, this was another creative project that the administration following mine did not continue.

The two grand conclaves during my administration were also examples of the New Thrust we wanted for Omega, emphasizing a change in priorities moving our fraternity toward more effective participation in community life. As I stated in the *ORACLE* in the Fall 1972:

> The new conclaves like other aspects of Omega must continue to provide the environment for reassessment, evaluation, and program formulation. It must continue to be the main instrument that melds the talents and experiences of brothers across America into projects

and programs that together make a massive, concerned movement that is felt in the crevices of community life.

Omega Fraternity to Assemble America's Most Influential Blacks

AVERY

[illegible]

One of the many articles that appeared in the black press in 1971 announcing Omega's Grand Conclave to be held in Houston, Texas

Grand Basileus Avery with Founder, Brother Oscar J. Cooper, Founder Brother Edgar A. Love, and National Executive Secretary Brother H. Carl Moultrie at the 1971 Houston Conclave

The Houston Conclave was perhaps the finest example of this intent. We had some great national leaders participating in that conclave. Foremost among the leaders present were the two living Founders of Omega Psi Phi Fraternity, Inc., Bishop Edgar A. Love and Dr. Oscar J. Cooper. The national leaders included Roy Wilkins, head of the NAACP; Vernon Jordan, executive director of the National Urban league; George Wiley, executive director of the National Welfare Rights Organization; and Dr. Benjamin Mays, president emeritus of Morehouse College. In later years, Dr. Mays was chosen to deliver the eulogy at Martin Luther King's funeral. James T. Felder, South

Dr. Walter Ridley, Mr. and Mrs. Oscar J. Cooper, Brother Grand, Mr. and Mrs. Edgar A. Love, and Dr. Benjamin Mays at the Houston, Texas Grand Conclave, 1971

Brother Grand (far right) chatting with Brother Dr. Benjamin Mays; Brother Ellis Corbett, Past Grand Basileus, and Brother John Moore standing at left

Carolina State Legislator; Edward Lewis, publisher of Essence Magazine; Hobart Taylor, legal advisor to Presidents John F. Kennedy and Lyndon B. Johnson; and Dr. John L. Cashin, contestant for governor of Alabama against George Wallace, also participated as speakers at this conclave. Several very important programmatic resolutions were passed. We passed a resolution to help fight sickle cell anemia through the provision of financial support for research and other programs and moved to support programs to achieve welfare rights for the needy. We pushed for quality education for black children and put more emphasis on political education, voter registration, and equality in the political arena.

I made many speeches around the country during my tenure as Grand Basileus, particularly at district conferences and achievement week programs. My theme was a consistent one that encouraged the use of our talents in participating in community life and making a real difference by doing so.

A good example was the speech that I gave at the Fifth District Conference in Louisville, Kentucky in April 1971. At that time I said:

> Omega must turn its sights more fully on the challenge of social responsibility if it is going to continue to function successfully in the black communities of this nation. Organizations like ours that function in the black community must stand the test of relevancy and what I call fraternal accountability. We need to move into an unprecedented period of constructive activism with programs that have a positive and outreaching character, programs designed to get the maximum use out of the human resource skills we have in Omega.
>
> As I see it, this is no time for an organization of men fortunate enough to have college training, or to be getting college training, to see the major attack on problems in the black community as someone else's responsibility. If we do not show our concern by action, how long before the cancer of indifference begins to take effect upon our own destiny and the destiny of others close to us.

St. Louis To Entertain Omegas In 55th Conclave

The second Grand Conclave during my administration was held in St. Louis, Missouri. Brother Alvin West was the Grand Marshall. I continued my emphasis on themes that held meaning to the black community. That theme was: "Reassessment of Goals for Black Americans in a Democracy." I had some great national leaders participating in the conclave sessions. William Nix, State Supreme Court Justice in Pennsylvania; William J. Kennedy, III, president of North Carolina Mutual, one of America's largest black businesses; Earl Graves, publisher of *Black Enterprise*; Milt Johnson, a buyer for J. C. Penny Company; Dr. Hildras A. Poindexter, a world renowned black research bacteriologist; J. Otis Smith, assistant legal counsel for General Motors; Dr. Jerome Gresham, president of Barber-Scotia College; and Garth Reeves, editor and publisher of *The Miami Times* and former president of the National Negro Newspapers Association were among the array of distinguished business and political leaders that took part in our sessions. There were thousands of Omega men, their families, and friends who attended and benefited from this conclave. At each conclave I wanted to make sure we provided useable information and knowledge to those attending to help them to be more effective in carrying out the goals that we mandated in Omega.

During my administration as Grand Basileus, we chartered 67 undergraduate chapters, three intermediate chapters, and 28 graduate chapters. Overall, our total chapter strength increased 33% during those three years. The fraternity has since that time eliminated intermediate chapters as a chapter form. While they did not last, intermediate chapters were set up during the 1960s to accommodate those members of Omega who had graduated from a college or university, but were not ready to join a graduate chapter. It was thought that an intermediate chapter would give recent graduates time to acclimate to post-degree life. It is often not an easy thing for a young graduate to suddenly be thrust into a chapter made up of older Omega men with set ideas and high chapter financial demands.

I sought to make sure that in my tenure we centralized our efforts around our four cardinal principles. What we did in initiating Project Aspiration served as a shining example of our application of the Cardinal Principle of **Scholarship**, particularly as it impacted our youth. The aggressive work of our Charles E. Drew Scholarship Commission kept the fundamentals of good scholarship continually before the brotherhood. While the Cardinal Principle of **Uplift** can be viewed as a Christian principle, I saw it as one that linked our interests with the need for us to uplift the human welfare of those around us. Our drug education program, Project Uplift, and our Health-O-Rama project were shining examples of this. The Cardinal Principle of **Perseverance** in my view is one that must be manifest in all the projects we undertake and in all the responsibilities we assume. The determination to make the project work, to carry out a responsibility to fulfillment regardless of the challenges we face, is the manner in which we celebrate this great cardinal principle. Of course, along with the traits of integrity, honesty, respect for women and family, inherent in the Cardinal Principle of **Manhood**, I associate this principle closely with the need to always persevere in what we do.

Avery (center) with two of the Omega founders,
Brother Oscar Cooper and Bishop Edgar Love

During the three-year period of my administration, 1970–1973, I was selected by *Ebony* magazine as one of the 100 most influential blacks in America!

I would hope that my administration would always be seen and remembered as one that sought through new and viable programming to move Omega's energies and intellect more toward the real concerns of human life. I was privileged to have many private chats with two of the Beloved Founders of the Omega Psi Phi Fraternity, Inc., Brother Edgar A. Love and Brother Oscar J. Cooper. Those discussions were priceless to me. They gave critical definition to my fraternal philosophy. Brother Love was one of the most gracious men I have ever known. His strong but slightly raspy voice expounded dignity and strength of character. When he spoke, the Omega world listened!

I spent many evenings at Brother Cooper's home in Philadelphia. There was something else I silently admired about Brother Cooper. He was a doctor who served black people in a rundown section of attached homes. He lived in the middle of this area, though inside of his home was a veritable palace. He never sought to move. He was dedicated to serving the people of that area and letting them know by staying there that he was one of them. I was at Brother Cooper's bedside when he was in the hospital, when I knew his health was fading fast. He had a beautiful and loyal wife who loved him and always attended Omega functions with him.

One of the most pleasurable acts of my fraternal life occurred in December of 1972 in Baltimore at a testimonial honoring Bishop Love when I had the great privilege of presenting and pinning a 30-diamond studded pin on his lapel. On that occasion I said to the audience:

Brother Avery pinning Founder Brother Edgar A. Love

> This pin is the one thing we found that he does not have and we are giving it to him on behalf of all the brothers here and throughout the United States as an expres-

sion of our love and esteem, because we in Omega know what Bishop Love has meant to us throughout the years.

One of the saddest days of my life was on May 7, 1974 when I read a resolution at the funeral of our beloved Founder Bishop Love.

Whereas the right Reverend Edgar A. Love, retired Bishop of the Methodist Church and Co-Founder of the Omega Psi Phi Fraternity, Inc., departed this life on May 1, 1974 and

Whereas from a quiet young man attending Howard University in the early 1900s he had indicated then that his life would be touched by sparks of greatness and

Whereas in 1911, together with Dr. Ernest A. Just, Frank Coleman, and Oscar J. Cooper, he gave birth to the Omega Psi Phi Fraternity, Inc., and has since that time been a brilliant leader, a constant inspiration, and a faithful shepherd to the thousands of men who have sought the life of Omega and

Whereas, in spite of whatever else his obligations may have been, he has found the time to give to his fraternity and

Whereas his counsel and deep expression of love both in word and practice will be sorely missed throughout the fraternity,

Now, therefore, let it be resolved that the Right Reverend Edgar A. Love will live in everlasting memory of all Omega Men and be it further resolved that in this solemn hour we commend his soul to Almighty God and be it further resolved that we here and now dedicate ourselves to the principles that he so firmly espoused.

Done this day, May 7, 1974, in the City of Baltimore, Maryland, by the authority of the Omega Psi Phi Fraternity, Inc.

Bishop Love was a truly fascinating man and one of the most endearing that I have ever had the pleasure of knowing.

I also had the pleasure of spending some extremely valuable time through the years with some of our past Grand Basilei, who made significant impacts upon the history of our great organization. I met Brother Clarence Holmes, who was our Grand Basileus in 1918, at several grand conclaves in the 1950s including one in Denver, Colorado, his home, and another in Washington, D.C. Brother Holmes spent his tenure building upon the programs started by Brother Love and Brother Cooper.

Brother Atkins was the Grand Basileus of Omega Psi Phi Fraternity in 1922–1923. He initiated the system of district representatives, emphasized scholarship development, fraternal expansion, conducted a review of our constitution, revised the initiation ritual, and reorganized our national administrative office. He could have run for another term but, for reasons of his own, he decided not to do so.

Brother Julius S. McClain was our Grand Basileus from 1927 to 1929. He was an outstanding Grand Basileus, who served for three terms. He had a very progressive administration. He set up a quarterly reporting system, encouraged purchasing of chapter houses, and was instrumental in the formation of the National Panhellenic Council. I met him under circumstances that proved to be somewhat embarrassing to him. I was asked to attend an Achievement Week program in the late 1960s in Newburgh, New York. Brother McClain was the guest speaker. He did not know that I would be present and was planning to use a copy of a speech I had given a year previous at a program in one of the southern states. How surprised he was to see me. When he showed me the copy of the speech I told him to go ahead and use it with my blessings. He chose instead to make other remarks that were still very appropriate. We had a long visit about Omega. I found him to be a fine, dignified brother who, like Brother Holmes, chose to focus upon the programs mandated in Omega at the time and not create anything new.

Brother Lawrence A. Oxley, an outstanding administrator, was our Grand Basileus from 1933 to 1935. He had been a lieutenant in the United States Army and also held several important military positions in the War Department during and after World War II. He was appointed the chief advisor

Grand Basileus Avery at an Alpha Omega Chapter's Mardi Gras, shaking hands with Brother Lawrence Oxley, who served as Grand Basileus 1933–35

on Negro Affairs in the United States Department of Labor. He did a great job in the revival of inactive chapters and in encouraging work on the history of Omega. Brother Oxley and I became great friends, and he was a great supporter of the new programs that I initiated during my administration. I was deeply honored and saddened to attend his funeral and burial in the National Cemetery in Washington, D.C.

Brother Albert W. Dent was our Grand Basileus from 1937 to 1940. I first met him when he was president at Dillard University in New Orleans, Louisiana, and I was a national vice chairman of the United Negro College Fund's annual campaign. He was an outstanding administrator and used his expertise to improve the workings of our Supreme Council. He, too, conducted a revision of our fraternity's constitution. During his administration Dreer's history of Omega from 1911–1939 was published. Brother Dent was also an outstanding leader in the United Negro College movement during the 1950s and early 1960s.

I was a district representative when I first met Brother Z. Alexander Looby. He was one of our most aggressive and most civil rights-minded of our leaders. As our Grand Basileus in a conclave in 1945, he got the grand conclave to vote that the major programs for Omega be redirected to areas of social-economic concern and stressed educational equality, individual equality, political equality, and social parity. When I was Grand Basileus I was determined to expand the mandate passed in Brother Looby's administration in 1945 and place great emphasis upon matters of social welfare as they impact the black community.

Brother Grand with Brother H. Carl Moultrie at the Grand Conclave in St. Louis, when he was National Executive Secretary. Brother Moultrie, a lawyer, later resigned and became Chief Judge of the District of Columbia

During a good part of my administration as Grand Basileus, Brother H. Carl Moultrie was the executive director of the fraternity. Carl was a giant in the life of Omega, a huge, respected presence who, for many years, was a critical help to every national leader of the organization. He certainly was a valuable aide to me. He resigned in 1973 to become a federal judge in the Superior Court of the District of Columbia. I had the rare and special privilege of investing him with his robe at a special SRO hearing before a panel of judges in Washington, DC Brother Moultrie later became Chief Judge of that district. After his death, the District of Columbia had a new federal court building in the district named in his honor, the H. Carl Moultrie Building. While a judge, Carl wrote me a letter at the end of my tenure as Grand Basileus.

> Dear Jim:
>
> I wish to take this opportunity to express my deep appreciation for the leadership you brought to Omega during your tenure in office as Grand Basileus. No one is in a better position to attest to that fact than I am. History will record you as one of the great spirits of our fraternal life. No sincere person accomplishes all that he desires to, thus, I know that you did not reach all the goals you had in mind. I also know you gave to the fraternity excellent leadership and increased our image

immeasurably. Thanks for the opportunity to have worked with you.

Yours in Omega,
Carl

I received another letter from one of Omega's most respected men, Dr. William A. McMillan, who was then President of Rust College in Holly Springs, Mississippi. He wrote:

Dear Brother Avery:

This letter comes to express a deep sense of appreciation for me and thousands of other brothers of the Omega Psi Phi Fraternity for the quality of leadership which you gave to us over the past three years. We consider these years the golden age of our fraternity. You set standards and developed an image that will for years be remembered by our brotherhood.

Because of your dedication and exemplary brotherhood, I am confident that we will move forward rather than backward as we program for the future.

The last two conclaves carried the kind of content that made it worthwhile for any brother to sacrifice the time to attend. Not only were they educational and informative, but the panelists and other programs provided insight and inspiration to all of us who attended. There was a good balance between the business, educational, and social phases of our conclaves that others may use as stepping-stones for even greater progress.

Most sincerely and fraternally yours,
Brother W. A. McMillan

Those who read this autobiography may think that I am on an ego trip by including such complimentary letters. I don't feel that way. I sincerely tried my very best to make a positive difference through my leadership, and I am proud of what was done. It's a pleasure for me to know that great Omega men like Brother H. Carl Moultrie, who became Chief Judge of the District of Columbia, and Brother Dr. W. A. McMillam, then President of Rust College, recognized it. I want to be remembered for the good things that I was able to achieve in whatever I undertook.

As of October 2005, there are nine living past Grand Basilei who are still actively involved in fraternity life. The oldest is Herbert E. Tucker, Jr. , our 23rd Grand Basileus (1955–1958). I am the next oldest living Grand Basileus, the 28th, (1970–1973). Edward J. Braynon, Jr., our 30th Grand Basileus, is next. He served from 1976 to 1979. Burnel E. Coulon is our 31st Grand Basileus (1979 to 1982). Following him is L. Benjamin Livingston, our 32 Grand Basileus (1982 to 1984). Moses C. Norman, Sr., followed him. Norman is our 33rd Grand Basileus (1984 to 1990). C. Tyrone Gilmore is our 34th Grand Basileus (1990 to 1994). Dorsey C. Miller, our 35th Grand Basileus, followed Brother Gilmore and was our Grand from 1994 to 1998. Lloyd J. Jordan, our 36th Grand Basileus, served from 1998 to 2002. All of us who have had the distinguished opportunity to lead this great fraternity are still committed, dedicated Omega men who remain ready to assist and provide counsel to our esteemed current leader who is, as of this writing, Brother George H. Grace, our 37th Grand Basileus.

I have been very fortunate throughout my years in Omega to be a part of the fraternity's Second District, a five-state area that is known for its many corporate headquarters, its high technological and pharmaceutical presence, its many educational institutions, and its major financial center. It is an area with high population densities, multiple social problems, and countless challenges. Omega men who live and mature in this environment with successful careers have an added quality that shows up in their participation in fraternity life. I feel that the Second District is in good hands with the likes of men like our current District Representative, Brother Gregory Ackles, as well as his 1st Vice, Brother Marvin Dillard, and Public Relations Director, Brother Ron Moffitt, who work tirelessly together for the good of the Second District at all times. We see this in the kind of innovative thinking in our conferences and our workshop proposals for action. Our past district representatives (DRs) have shown this exceptional intelligent insight and initiative in what they have achieved.

Brother Marvin C. Dillard, First Vice District Representative 2004–2006, and Mrs. Robin Dillard

Brother Gregory E. Ackles, Second District Representative 2004–2006, and Mrs. Beverly Ackles

Brother Ronald J. Moffitt, Second District Director of Public Relations 1994–2006, and Mrs. Andrea "Angie" Moffitt

XX

More Educating and More Education

In 1971, in order to broaden my management skills, I was selected by Humble to attend an executive management course in the Graduate School of Business Administration of the University of Southern California. This was an outstanding experience that was shared with business executives from all over the world and from several United States corporations. It sharpened my intellectual grasp of a variety of business problems and trends. Interestingly, it was my first exposure to the term downsizing, which actually did not become prominent in big business operations until the late 1990s. Business schools, like the one I attended, were certainly on top of emerging trends. This management training improved my ability to be an effective manager for Humble.

I had a great time that summer at the University of Southern California. I never worked so hard on courses. The number of books we had to read each week was astounding, not leaving time for much leisure activities, until the end of the program, when we played golf at a course outside of the Rose Bowl. At the close of our executive training, our graduating ceremonies were held at the historic El Dorado Hotel in San Diego, California.

HUMBLE APPOINTS JAMES S. AVERY REGION PUBLIC AFFAIRS MANAGER

In 1971, the company changed the emphasis of our activities dealing with the various publics.

The increase in environmental concern for cleaner air and water as well as the growing pressures on government to take greater interest in occupational safety and oil and gas supply and demand, caused the oil industry to realize that public relations was becoming more like public affairs. Thus, the change in the name and the emphasis of the work we were doing from public relations to public affairs. Some months later, I was promoted from Public Relations Manager to Public Affairs Manager. While our region remained the same in terms of the territory covered, the entire country was divided up into six public affairs regions. We had greater status as managers and were practically considered like regional vice presidents. This assignment in 1971was one of the highest positions of any black in the oil industry.

Several years later in 1975, I was selected by *Who's Who in America* to be listed in their annual publication. (Now 30 years later, because of my involvement in higher education and in fraternal affairs I am still listed each year.) I am also listed in *Who's Who in Black America* and while an executive with Esso/ Exxon, I was listed in *Who's Who in Finance and Industry.*

The early seventies were most challenging for us in the petroleum industry, particularly in relation to oil and gas supply. We faced boycotts, bomb threats and countless media calls about the assumptions of restricting supply and price gouging. We made countless media visits throughout the region and responded to hundreds of calls. I was on radio a number of times responding to questions about oil operations. We made personal visits to key legislators in our region. We made hundreds of visual-aids presentations and speeches around the region to organizations and clubs about oil and gas development and explaining the oil and gas situation in the United States.

During this period, I went to Chicago to attend the McCann-Erickson School for handling communications on TV and Radio to learn how to handle ourselves better before the camera under extreme pressure. We spent a week being taught how to respond in ways that bridged the replies to what we wanted to say about a problem or issue. We learned to be more focused with our responses. In the early stages of the training classes, they tried to make you angry or confused to determine how you would handle the situation. I remember when I first sat down for a mock TV interview, the first thing I was asked was, "How did it feel to be the Head Nigger in charge?" Well, I successfully kept my cool although I really wanted to say, "You bastard, what did you call me?" While I did not appear ruffled by his comment, I did not have a good answer for him. I simply said, "It feels damn good!" Some of the guys really got ruffled when they were asked a sensitive question. One of the vice presidents was asked if he was a homosexual just to get a rise out of him, and he really got mad and did not want to go on with the mock interview. It was a terrific course and I learned a great deal, including how to do a short, effective TV spot on a problematic situation.

XXI

Guiding Exxon's Public Affairs in the 1970s

Getting back to my position with Exxon, the seventies were very challenging years, particularly regarding energy supply. Many of our public affairs activities centered on this subject. During the 1970s, the supply of oil was less than normal, principally due to OPEC countries cutting back on production. The general public did not realize that the flow of oil had to be steady through the entire system. Imagine the supply of oil coming through a pipeline that goes from the wellhead to storage through shipment to refineries for processing and then by tanker truck to the dealer. Whenever there was a shortage of as little as 4% of the oil from the pipeline, there was a problem in the supply at the consumer end. When that occurred, there were long lines at service stations. Customers would run out of oil to heat their homes or run their businesses. The media made us look like the bad guys. We were picketed and blasted in the press and on TV. There was one occasion when a live bomb was delivered to our regional office (where I had my office) in Pelham, New York. The New York City bomb squad had to come and remove it and detonate it. I cannot tell you the number of times I had to speak to the media, even on radio, to explain that we did not have ships sitting out in the outer harbors waiting for the prices to go higher. We were not doing anything to cause supply problems. Those years were extremely busy times for us. Being the largest energy company in the world, we were the targets for the frustration that the public felt.

Interestingly, to be fully engulfed in matters dealing with public affairs and oil industry concerns in general and not focusing on racially related matters was not a major stretch for me. I knew what my job was, and I had studied all aspects of it. I knew I wanted to be the very best public affairs manager the company had and this required a mainline attitude and mainline thinking to handle mainline situations. Handling all kinds of problems was part of it.

I made some changes in staff area responsibilities. I put Bob Haslam in the Boston office so that we would have a person in the New England region on hand for any situation. Barry Woods, a bright young man who management planned to move along, joined us from sales, and I asked him to spend most of his time on community and press relations. Al Sitarski, who was based in New Jersey, took care of our government relations activities in New Jersey, New York, and Pennsylvania. Jack McDonald joined us from Esso Research to take over Pennsylvania. Ken Smith was our staff media and community relations expert. He was also in charge of the production of booklets and was assigned to take the lead in the production of TV tapings. He was invaluable to me. I always had the highest respect for his abilities. One of his most important jobs was planning and directing video presentations of what we did in the Northeastern Region for our Houston headquarters.

During the 1970s particularly, one of the primary public affairs objectives in the oil industry was to help the public understand the oil shortage and the need for the United States to take action to become more self-sufficient. In 1977, I gave a speech to the New York State Council for the Social Studies, Council on Social Education, that was published in the fall issue of their *Social Studies Record*. I pointed out that the United States would remain dependent on oil and gas for about two-thirds of our total energy supply needs for many years. This prediction included our industry

Jim Avery (middle) at Exxon working with Ken Smith and Bob Haslam, members of his Public Affairs staff

Jim Avery and the Exxon Tiger

forecast for the development of alternate forms of energy. The problem was and remains today that our country's oil and gas production has not kept pace with the continued growth in the demand for energy. At that time, we were consuming nearly twice as much oil in the United States as we were producing and ten times as much as we were finding. The only way we have been able to take care of our energy needs is to increase the importation of oil from foreign countries. I concluded that speech as I did many others I gave on the energy supply problem by stating:

> Our nation has a serious long-term energy problem. Consequently, we must develop and adhere to conservation programs that will permit continued economic growth even as we endeavor to moderate our energy consumption. This means a national energy policy that will encourage all energy enterprises to put forth a maximum effort. It means enlisting rather than frustrating the effort of all of us who can contribute. We need to develop an informed, enlightened citizenry that has a sense of the challenge and some understanding of the basic energy situation we face.

It was a sobering fact to realize that much of what we would need through the next century would have to come from oil and gas resources we had not yet discovered! This was one of the principle reasons for us to push for the right to explore for oil and gas on the Atlantic Outer Continental Shelf. To do this we had to get approval from the various states along the East Coast, not only to put bases for exploration on land along the coast, but to drill for oil off their coastline. There were three areas off the East Coast where we would want to drill for oil: the Georges Bank off the New England coast; the Baltimore

Canyon off the Mid-Atlantic coast' and in the South Atlantic off the Carolinas, Georgia, and Florida. The American Petroleum Institute's Offshore Subcommittee had the job of getting the approval. In 1977, I was asked to be the Vice-Chairman of Public Affairs for the American Petroleum Institute's Offshore Subcommittee. The priority objective of this sub-committee was to get witnesses to testify before governmental agencies and to provide support statements to those agencies to seek the right to carry out the drilling. We were successful in getting approval for the drilling in each of the targeted areas. I personally took media representatives and other officials out to the drill ship in the Baltimore Canyon. We did the same off the Georges Bank and in the South Atlantic. Unfortunately, none of the drilling for oil and gas was successful. I saw core samples from these drillings, and they were all solid rock with no hint of oil or gas in them. Being Vice-Chairman of this API Subcommittee was a great experience that unfortunately did not help the United States become more energy self-sufficient.

During the 1970s, I was very involved in oil industry affairs in other positions too. Not only was I closely associated with all of the state petroleum councils in the company's Northeastern Region, I chaired the New York State Petroleum Council's Executive Committee for two years. In that position I worked with representatives of the oil and gas companies that operated in that state in educating the public on energy matters. During this time, I also served as chairman of the New York State Business Council's Energy Committee.

For several years in the 1970s, I was a member of the New York State Traffic Safety Council, an organization that served as the public conscience on safety matters in the state. I was also a member of the New York State Council on Economic Education and the New Jersey State Council on Economic Education. Both organizations sought to increase the importance of teaching economic education in the high schools in each state.

XXII

More Challenges

During the time I was in the Pelham, New York, office, my secretary got married and resigned. In seeking someone to take her place I hired Joan Horrigan to be my executive secretary in our regional public affairs department. Joan proved to be an outstanding addition to our staff and ran the office with great efficiency.

After almost four years of working closely together, I could feel the relationship between Joan and me getting more and more personal. I was reticent about asking her out because of my position at Exxon. It was in 1976 that Joan finally suggested we go to dinner. We were falling in love without either of us saying it. At that time, I was beginning to know Joan's three children as they came to the office after school to pick up their mother from work. We became engaged in the late summer of 1976 and understandably Joan had to retire. It was not proper for a manager and his secretary to be in a romantic relationship at that time.

We spent a lot of time together the remainder of that year. Joan's children and mine were getting to know each other both in Pelham and Scotch Plains, New Jersey. There were evening hours that we would spend sitting on a bench down by the Long Island Sound. I was really smitten with her beauty, her personality, and her character and when I got home I would put my thoughts down in writing. On one occasion I wrote:

> It was like a moving ballet, one that I really was not totally conscious of, yet, I knew it was there. The softly lapping sound of the waves, a silent sailboat moving by with quiet dignity, a water skier crisscrossing in

the wake of his guiding boat. People were walking by now and then, almost as if invading or intruding on a moment too precious to share with anyone else.

Joan and I knew that we were in an interracial relationship that was not something that all people would accept. I think people in Pelham, even some of her relatives, including her mother, thought Joan was out of her mind for encouraging a relationship with me. Our feelings for each other had to be genuine and immense to overshadow such concerns. I wrote about this situation too:

One should not be frightened with inaction simply because we do not already hold the answers to all the specific questions that we will have to deal with. There simply is no way to charter the details of our future in advance. Those who demand a complete picture of the future will never be the ones to shape it. Tomorrow will belong to those who are willing to follow an instinct, to express a feeling, to pursue a dream, and to choose a course destined for them. Commitment to a cause is ultimately based upon faith in a vision that one has for oneself and society and not in dispassionate calculations and reams of facts and figures. How much does one need to know, to know what they want? We want to participate in decisions that affect our lives. We want to live without fear. We want to feel that what we do and who we are has meaning for ourselves and for those who we care for. We want to count for something and we want to know that there is a reason for our being alive. We have that opportunity regardless of what others may think.

On another occasion after spending time together, I wrote:

You are a very stabilizing, motivating, comforting influence in my life, an influence that I need without qualification or reservation. It is something that lifts my heart, eases my burdens, and keeps any ideas that generate

> anxiety or apprehension from coming into my being. Your love, your way, your words give me the strength I need to be what I am and what I can be in the face of whatever lies ahead.

One evening after spending several hours together when I got home, I wrote about my feelings:

> It is almost torturous to be so blissfully happy one day and night and then experience the isolation of being so alone and so very lonely the next. Like the comparison of "all that's best in dark and bright" with everything that's wrong with the world, I only know I miss you so very much when I'm not with you. I pray that God will give you the courage and the strength to endure and to do what you know must be done now. It was said some time ago that courage is the price that life exhorts from us for granting us peace. The person that does not know courage knows no release from even the little things. You must manifest that courage. At the same time know that our relationship was born of a love not forced, but one that seemed to rise out of heaven with the blessings of God, unmasked and unsought. I only want our love to continue to grow and grow, if more growth is possible, and mature with an unmatched beauty and companionship. I want this more and more each day. That is why tonight I ask God for strength and patience during this period of time.

We were married in January of 1977 in a quaint little church in Westwood, New Jersey, with many friends from the Exxon office, Joan's children and mine, and other family members attending the ceremony. Andre Smith, who was a minister, and who also worked in the personnel department of Exxon in the Pelham office, married us. His wife was the church organist. We chose him because he was a beautiful man of God and a minister of this lovely little church. Following the marriage we had a wonderful reception at the Swiss Chalet. Ken Smith of my staff was best man, and he gave a wonderful toast. Joan's cousin, Lianne Birkhold, who flew in from California, was the maid of honor. Every one who attended, family and friends alike, had a fun time at our wedding reception.

Jim and Joan Avery at the Omicron Chi Chapter's James S. Avery Annual Scholarship Ball, 1999

Following the wedding, Joan sold her house in Pelham and moved with two of her children, Jean and Bobby, into my house on Inverness Drive in Scotch Plains, New Jersey. George, her older son, graduated from Pelham High School and went to live with his father in Illinois before starting college at Western Illinois University. My son Jim, Jr., who was 17, still lived at home. Sheryl, my daughter, was living in Paterson and was attending William Patterson College. We had decided not to try the patience of the people of Pelham by moving to Joan's house. Scotch Plains was a more hospitable location and I had been living there for nine years. All the kids got along well together. Bobby and Jean were free of any prejudice and there never was any problem about territorial rights or anything else. No one could have asked for anything more. All the children accepted people based of the content of their character not the color of their skin. I love her kids as I do mine with a love and a respect that is overwhelming. I am sure that George, Joan's oldest son would have demonstrated the same wonderful character traits had he lived with us. Like Jean and Bobby, he too was right at home when he came to visit. George and Jimmy got along in great style and would often go out together when George was in New Jersey. I am sure, as far as the girls were concerned, they took no prisoners!

Naturally, there were the usual trials and tribulations of bringing up teenagers and sending kids off to college, but we managed to live through it. Joan and I were asked by some of our white and black friends if our children had any problem with our interracial marriage or their merging together as family members. Our children have never expressed any negative attitudes about our marriage or about being in an interracial situation. All of our children seemed to have a positive chemistry with each other and with being a part of a family. When I had a heart attack and needed open heart surgery at St. Joseph's Hospital in Paterson, all five children and their respective spouses converged at the hospital to be with me. That in itself gave me the will to survive this traumatic event.

I have always tried to be a part of the lives of all the children and later of the grandchildren. I attended graduations, participated in the weddings, shared the good and unhappy times, and gave advice and money when needed. I always wanted to live my life so that Joan's children as well as my own would respect me as a father and as a man who tried to make a positive difference in the world around him. That is how I wanted it and that is how it shall be as long as I live.

Joan and I have often been asked what challenges we have faced as an interracial couple. Years ago, this kind of relationship was definitely frowned upon in many circles, both black and white. With the passing of years, this distinction in social situations is much more blurred than when we were first married. There were occasions of subtle bigotry and prejudice, but we have been so in love that we just didn't care about what others thought. I have always believed that you have to relate to people on a one-to-one basis regardless of race, creed, or color. Whatever the problems, they were never insurmountable for either one of us.

As I mentioned earlier, Joan and I were married in January 1977. Three years later, Exxon headquarters in Houston closed the Pelham, New York, office, where the Regional Public Affairs office had been located and moved the entire regional office staff to West Norwalk, Connecticut. Joan and I and the last two children, Bob and Jean, moved from Scotch Plains, New Jersey to a beautiful home in West Norwalk. Unbeknownst to all of us who had moved up to Connecticut, Exxon headquarters in Houston, Texas, had decided to phase out the regional office location in Connecticut over a period of three to four years and consolidate these administrative marketing functions in Houston, Texas. Hundreds of lives were affected by this decision to first move from Pelham, New York, to West Norwalk, and then later to eliminate the office entirely.

It was ironic that earlier in 1980 I had presented a proposal to headquarters to reorganize the entire public affairs function in the Northeast, linking all the marketing and refining into one office, which would be located in North Jersey with several satellite locations. It was that proposal that the headquarters administration in Houston adopted. By the time it was done, I had already moved to Connecticut. I decided not to take early retirement at that time and opted to go on what they called the Exxon Loaned Executive Program to a not-for-profit organization in New York City called COMP, the Council of Municipal Performance. COMP was a national not-for-profit organization whose mission was to promote management efficiency and fiscal accountability in local government. At COMP we held a number of conferences and meetings with local officials from various communities around the nation dealing with such topics as waste man-

Jim Avery and Dr. John Marlin, President of the Council on Municipal Performance, coauthors of the Book of American City Rankings

agement, fiscal accountability, and municipal security (a topic today of major national significance). We also put out booklets on these important subjects. The COMP Board was comprised of some prominent New Yorkers including a mayoral candidate, financier Jim Laventhal, a major player in the municipal bond business, one of the Rockefeller brothers, and the Dean of the Columbia University School of Business. I enjoyed the experience and while there I co-authored a book with the president of COMP, Dr. John Marlin, entitled the *Book of American City Rankings*. In commenting on the book, the publisher noted that it was a listing first!

> Never before had so many facts about the nation's principle cities been brought together in a single book. It is a useful compilation of comprehensive, carefully selected facts and figures about the quality of life and performance of the nation's 100 largest cities, where one-half of all Americans live or work. The book's 300 tables cover a wide variety of subjects, from population and pollution to religion, politics, city finance, and the arts and leisure. In selecting data for inclusion, the authors have focused on areas of broad public concern about cities and compared what cities are like to live in, what their trends are, and how good a job city government is doing. The *Book of American City Rankings* will pique your curiosity and shake your perceptions and expand your knowledge about America's vital urban centers.

The statistical tables we used in the book showed what cities were the sunniest, the fastest growing, which had the highest tax rates, the lowest cost of living, which were ethnically the most homogeneous, which had the most retirees, the best public transportation, and the best educated work force.

The book contained a host of other interesting and pertinent facts. The book received excellent reviews in several magazines and on television on the Merv Griffin Show. Shortly after its publication, the book was featured in the magazine that United Airlines puts in the reading slot in front of each of the seats on all of their planes. Personally, I did not receive any revenue from the book since I was on executive loan to COMP from Exxon and was paid by Exxon.

In 1983, I left the Council of Municipal Performance and went back to Exxon as Senior Public Affairs Consultant, a position I held until I retired in August of 1986 after 31 years in the oil industry.

I have also been asked if there has been anything I sought but never achieved, and I can honestly say that it has always been the journey, not the destination, that was important in my life. Someone once said that my psyche was under-girded with the spirit of being driven and highly focused on the objectives I faced in life. Maybe so. To do the very best I could, at whatever I was doing, has been my ultimate goal.

Joan and I moved back to New Jersey in the fall of 1983, back to the same area in Scotch Plains where we had lived before moving to Connecticut. We could have remained in Connecticut, but I felt that I would be better off in Scotch Plains in pursuing future endeavors. Joan went to work at Muhlenberg Regional Medical Center, where she remained until she retired.

While all of this was going on in my personal life, I was still doing things out in the broad community. During the 1970s, Exxon had been providing educational funding support to a regional intervention organization located in Philadelphia called PRIME, Inc. In the late 1970s, I was elected to the board of PRIME. This organization was a not-for-profit one that worked with selected class groups in Philadelphia and Camden secondary schools. The classes were made up of youngsters specially selected by each school to be in what they called Prime Classes. The idea was to take students with high educational promise and give them additional educational training to better prepare them for college and subsequent jobs in business and industry. Corporations provided the financial support for a small staff based in Philadelphia that coordinated the program with the various high schools, arranged the visits to business locations, as well as, arranging the summer study programs at local universities and colleges such as Villanova University, University of Pennsylvania, and Drexel University. The board was responsible for overseeing the entire program. I enjoyed being a part of PRIME, Inc., and particularly being involved in an organization that assisted young people in getting an outstanding educational foundation that got them into the finest colleges and universities in the country. What a thrill each year to have graduates of this program come up to me and tell me they were chemists, engineers, moving into administration and going for their MBAs. I assumed the vice chairmanship in 1989 and remained in that position until 1992 when I decided to resign from the PRIME organization. Two years later, I was astounded to hear that PRIME, Inc., did not receive the necessary funding to continue. I believe that part of the reason was that the National Science Foundation came into the city with a program that absorbed much of the need to provide support and enrichment studies for these promising students.

During that period of time, Joan's son George Horrigan graduated from Western Illinois University and later graduated from law school in California and became an attorney. He eventually set up a law firm with his partner Curtis Floyd in Bakersfield, California. He and his wife, Lisa, have two children, George III and Emily. Jean, Joan's daughter, also graduated from Western Illinois University and, after a career in retail management, married Bob Gregus and they have two sons, Peter and John. Joan's son Bob graduated from Iowa State University and has a managerial position with a retail corporation and has one daughter, Amy.

My daughter, Sheryl, has two children, Kenny and Kelly. Kenny attended the University of Maryland and Kelly went to Montclair State University. Kenny, an all-star back in high school in South Brunswick, New Jersey, played on the varsity football team at the University of Maryland. Kelly, an outstanding softball player, played shortstop on the highly rated Montclair State University team while she was there.

My son, Jim, Jr., had two boys from a marriage to Natalie Pierce. The older boy is Steven and the younger one is Kevin.

After the marriage fell apart, both boys went to live with Jim in Florida. Kevin is in high school and has become an outstanding athlete. Steven is at a local college in Florida at the time of this writing. Jim is working in airport security and is doing a good job of raising two teenage boys, despite the fact that he had to do it by himself.

Joan Avery's son George Horrigan, his wife Lisa, and their two children, Emily and George III

Joan's son Bobby with his daughter, Amy, and fiance, Lisa McLaughlin

Joan Avery's daughter Jean Gregus with her husband, Robert, and their two sons, Peter and John.

Brother Grand with Joan, Jim's granddaughter Kelly Avery, his grandson Kenny Rogers, and daughter Sheryl at Iota Xi Chapter's Elders Honor

Brother Grand with grandsons Steven and Kevin, sons of Jim, Jr.

James Avery, Jr. with his friend Leone

XXIII

Speeches and Honors

The meeting of the Grand Basilei: Brother Jim Avery, Grand Basileus of Omega Psi Phi Fraternity, Inc. and Dr. Deborah Cannon Partridge Wold, Grand Basileus of Zeta Phi Beta Sorority, Inc.; both hale from Cranford, NJ

Jim Avery with two brothers, Friend and Louis, and sister Alice

In October of 1986, I had the distinct honor of being invited to be the keynote speaker for the Cranford First Baptist Church's 100th Anniversary celebration. It is one of the oldest, if not the oldest Baptist church, in New Jersey, and its current minister is a fine young man named Rev. Alfred E. Brown, Jr., a member of a prominent Cranford family. I was introduced that day by a wonderful friend, Dr. Deborah Cannon Partridge

Wolfe, associate minister of First Baptist, one of the most dynamic women I have ever known. She had been a Grand Basileus of Zeta Phi Beta Sorority, education chief for a House of Representatives Committee, a professor at Queens College, and adjunct instructor at numerous other universities. Deborah had received many honorary doctorates. She is undoubtedly one of the most decorated, celebrated, and honored black women to ever live in America.

My comments at the church celebration centered upon our responsibility as parents and responsible citizens not to sweep the concerns and problems of youth aside. We owe it to our children and to youth in general to listen, to talk, to reason, to be involved as family and as friends. It is on the local level, in our homes, our neighborhoods, and our towns, that each one of us can make our presence felt to a degree that really matters. I remember telling the youngsters, "Don't let anybody's low expectation of you cause you to believe it! In everything you do, do it the very best way you can. Live each day so that only the very best is good enough."

It was something special to be a part of that anniversary celebration and to have my sister and my two remaining brothers in attendance.

In November of 1997, I was invited to speak at the Achievement Week program conducted by the Xi Iota Iota Chapter of Omega Psi Phi Fraternity in the Troy, Sidney, Piqua, and Lima area of Ohio. To me, that program set the standard for such activities. It was a general community event that involved the four mayors of all four communities, state legislative representatives, educational officials from state and local levels, and included community leadership from a host of groups and organizations. I could see the great respect that the broad community had for my brothers in that chapter and their activities. Brother Jarrett A. Thomas was Basileus of Xi Iota Iota that year, and both he, Brother Ronald Humphrey, and other members of the chapter left no stone unturned. The scholarship awards, the keys from the four cities, the visits to other chapter activities in the Dayton area made the entire experience unforgettable. Brother Thomas and his wife Ruth were extremely gracious hosts for my visit.

In 1998, while still living in North Edison, I was selected with a group of ten others to be inducted in the Cranford Sports Hall of Fame. Our pictures were placed in a special "Wall of Fame" area of the main hall of the high school gymnasium. I felt very proud of that honor since I had spent many years at that school as a student, a teacher, adviser, and coach.

Jim Avery in the Cranford High School's gym, next to his photo on the school's WALL OF FAME, containing pictures of all those inducted into the school's Hall of Fame

Brother Lance Wilson presents an award to Brother Avery

Brother Grand with Brother Milt Johnson, chair of the 1999 Elders Honors Program

In February of 1999, I was honored at one of the best planned, sophisticated, and professionally conducted programs that I have ever attended. It was organized by Iota Xi Chapter, New York City. It was an ELDERS HONOR DINNER DANCE, where I received that chapter's 1999 Iota Xi Elders Honor Award. I have never felt more honored, more touched by the way the brothers in that chapter displayed their fraternal love for service and leadership to Omega. It was an added privilege for me to have past Grand Basileus Tyrone C. Gilmore and Grand Keeper of Records and Seal, Brother Terrel D. Parris, attend with Brothers Rudy Powell, Eddie Taylor, and Nathan Thomas, past honorees. To have received this recognition from such superb brothers in Omega such as Milt Johnson, Lance Wilson, Derrick Hostler, chapter basileus then, Arnold Eagle, Neil Philips, Joe Sanders, and Dan Bythewood, was one of the highest accolades in my life in Omega. Iota Xi's Elders Honors Program broke the mold for such events!

Brothers Nate Thomas and Eddie Taylor join Brother Avery as past Elder winners

Brother Grand with a few Second District Representatives

In the year 2000, I was honored by being selected along with six other former Cranfordites to receive an award from the Cranford Fund for Educational Excellence and the Cranford High School Alumni Awards Committee for significant contributions over the years in education and community endeavors. This award was very special to me since it came from an outstanding group of Cranford citizens led at the time by Carol Dreyer. At the award dinner I was extremely happy to have my wife, daughter, stepson, granddaughter, nieces, and friends to share the evening with me. I was honored to have Joan Vicci, a former student of mine, introduce me. In expressing my thanks, I said:

> I want to express my appreciation for this recognition and for what the Cranford Fund for Educational Excellence is doing to support meaningful innovating projects in the Cranford Public Schools. Those of us who are honored here tonight have all taken essentially different roads using basically the same tools of education to guide our way. In each instance, however, it has not been a road that has been traveled alone. On occasions like tonight, I think back on those defining moments in my life…those events, circumstances, and people who have made a positive impact upon me and shaped the design of my life. When I was a student in Cranford High School, I had teachers who never let me forget that I could achieve my goal of going to Columbia University on an academic scholarship. Through this kind of support and encouragement one becomes better able to face life's challenges and to seize opportunities that can make a difference in the world around us. I had such opportunities during my years of teaching and coaching at Cranford High School, I had them as a former business executive with Exxon, and I have them still in my current statewide educational responsibilities.

Two other occasions must be included among those that one never forgets. In early April, 2005, my fraternity chapter,

Omicron Chi Basileus Mo Lucky and second District Rep. Greg Ackles

Omicron Chi, gave me an 82nd Birthday Celebration. It brought together brothers from many of Omega's chapters and districts along with family members and other friends. It was a very humbling experience for me and one of the happiest and most memorable. In response to the receipt of many gifts and accolades, I said:

> I am blessed with my membership in an organization not only founded by great men, but based on some of the greatest principles of living. I am blessed with a wonderful family that is well represented here today. My wife Joan has been a special blessing to me. We have been married almost 30 years and I am sincere when I tell you that whatever I have done, whatever decision I have made, she has had a very positive and beneficial impact on all of it. I have always felt Omega Psi Phi Fraternity to be a very special kind of organization. Not only one that gathers the very best quality of mankind, but an organization that was designed by its Founders to be an effective body in the communities where we live. I have felt that way since the very first time that I learned all the history and past achievements of Omega men. I will never forget when I opened my eyes and

saw the beautiful escutcheon before me in the glow of soft candlelight. It left an indelible Omega imprint on my soul.

When I became a Basileus in Omicron Chi Chapter, I thoroughly enjoyed having our chapter do the things mandated for us. When I become a DR, I wanted to make sure our district, which has always been a major brain cell for Omega, continually tested itself against our vows and as a result come up with programming designed at battling some of the major social concerns that faced our communities. The mandated Shirtsleeve Conference, which I started in 1965, is one of the prime examples.

In my years as Grand Basileus, I had the opportunity to lead our fraternity in a major national crusade on key issues like drug education, education of our youth, public housing, health, scholarships, and chapter development. In addition, the conclaves, during my administration, dealt with important national concerns and were serious learning experiences for the brothers. And, I handpicked a great team to work with me. I am so proud of those years that heightened Omega's presence and effectiveness on the national scene. I ended my remarks at my 82nd Birthday Celebration by saying:

> It has been my honor and my responsibility as an Omega man to continue to do whatever I can to give depth and broad meaning to what our organization is charged to do. We all know that we live in an imperfect world and that is a major reason I continue to admonish all men of Omega to respect our organization, to live up to the vows we took, and to make a real difference in the lives we live.
>
> To me there is no greater fraternity to serve mankind in so many effective ways. Brothers of Omega, let us never forget that this high level of responsibility requires the best of men, not those who just want to wear the colors, or join for selfish motives, but men who lead the way to defy and abhor weakness, detest dishonesty, and scorn immorality. It requires strong men who use

Clyde Allen, Executive Director of NAMD, presents the President's Award to Jim Avery

their four principles as swords and plowshares to beat away the chaff of indifference and discord and all other obstacles that stand in the way of greatness.

Birthdays are important events in the lives of all of us. But I want this one to mark a day of special promise when each Omega man professes anew to blot out all imperfections that seek to make their way into our fold and to recommit to standing tall for Omega. May all of us continue to be the examples of Love, Cooper, Coleman, and Just, linked soul to soul, merging our interest in a common cause, encircled by a friendship that can never die, a friendship that will last longer than forever.

May the blessings of a loving God continue to guide your way. Thank you so very much for the honors you have bestowed upon me. May God grant me the privilege of doing all I can to continue to earn your respect and love.

Jim Avery with other 2005 NAMD Honorees (left to right): Fred Jones, Jr., Founder of the Southern Heritage Classic, Carol H. Williams, President/CEO of Carol H. Williams Advertising, and Kelvin Boston, President of Boston Media Group, Inc.

Later in April, Clyde Allen, Executive Director of the National Alliance of Market Developers, Inc. (NAMD), invited me to come to Cleveland, Ohio to attend the 2005 Annual Conference. This is the same organization for which I served as president from 1964 through 1966 and board chairman in 1967. I am the oldest living national officer of this organization and they wanted to acknowledge my participation in those historic years by presenting me with the President's Award.

Membership in NAMD in those early years was largely made up of representatives from corporations that held jobs that served the Black community. It was a great pleasure in 2005, some 40 years later, to find that most of the current members are entrepreneurs with their own businesses serving not only the Black community but the general one as well. I found NAMD not only to be alive and well, but doing an increasingly significant job in the business life of America.

In my remarks, after receiving the President's Award, I said:

> May I express my thanks to all the members of the National Alliance of Market Developers, Inc., for this honor. It is a real privilege to be with you today and I am deeply grateful.
>
> As I look back on my 31 years of corporate life that began in 1956, I can reflect upon some wonderful and challenging experiences dealing with energy development and its supply, and with customer understanding or lack of understanding. But, no experiences during that time were more interesting and important in many ways than my years of association with NAMD. Those years were wonderful and challenging as well.
>
> Those who had responsibility for what was then called the "Negro Market" had to work within society's shapes and forms of discrimination and segregation that existed within the communities we served as well as in the corporate structure. In those days we spent as much time educating internal management as we did carrying out our business responsibilities.
>
> Many of those in sales often operated on a shoestring budget with little real central office concern and little or no real technical support. That, of course, is one

of the key reasons why the formation of NAMD was so important.

I was not on hand in 1954 when this organization was formed; I came on the scene in 1956 when Tennessee A&I was still the focus of our organized life. That is where those of us who could travel nationally at that time went to participate in the career conference in the spring. And subsequently, that is where we began our annual marketing conferences. Moss Kendricks of Coca-Cola, Ted Lassiter of IBM, Clarence Holte of BBD&O, Leroy Jeffries of Johnson Publications, Louise Prothro of Pet Milk, Herb Wright of Phillip Morris, along with Joe Albright, Frankie Dee, and Herbie Whiteman were names that come to mind among the key figures present in those early days of NAMD. Those early conferences in many ways fulfilled the need for technical support and up-to-date marketing information.

I like to think that today, I am speaking for all of the market developers of those days when I say to you thank you for continuing this important alliance and for giving it broader definition and significance as a market-place organization. Best wishes for continued success.

Again, thank you for this unforgettable honor.

My trip to Cleveland, Ohio to be with today's members of NAMD was a great pleasure. I hope I will have the opportunity to attend future conferences of this important organization.

When I reflect on the honors that have come my way, I realize how fortunate and blessed I have been, not only to have experiences like these, but to be remembered years later for what was done at that time. Those "pats on the back" keep me focused and genuinely serve to further energize my spirit and to help me continue to live in caring and responsible ways.

XXIV

Appointments in Higher Education

Education, especially higher education, over the years has been a matter of great interest to me. That interest has become even more profound in today's world. There are good reasons why this should be a concern for all right-thinking people. Never before in our nation's history has education, especially post-secondary education, been so directly related to income and standard of living. Increasing numbers of citizens primarily members of so-called minority groups and those in educationally and economically disadvantaged environments are doomed to static, if not decreasing, standards of living if denied the benefits of access and opportunity to quality education including higher education. In succinct terms, the well-being of those without post-secondary educational opportunities have been in a free fall with their prospects for a better life deteriorating more rapidly than ever before. This is why I was so excited when in 1993 Jim Florio, the Governor of the State of New Jersey, appointed me to the State of New Jersey Educational Opportunity Fund Board of Directors and also to the Student Assistance Board. The Educational Opportunity Fund (EOF) was created in 1968 when Tom Kean was governor. EOF is one of America's most comprehensive and successful state-supported efforts to ensure higher educational opportunity for capable, highly motivated students who come from backgrounds of educational and economic disadvantage.

In partnership with New Jersey's colleges and universities, EOF carries out this collaborative effort through the EOF Board of Directors, which administers the program, and the

New Jersey Professional Association of EOF staffers who are employed at the New Jersey's 28 public and 13 independent colleges and universities. The Board sets policy, approves all necessary regulations for the program's operation, develops the annual budget request for the statewide program, and supports EOF programs at the New Jersey public and independent colleges and universities that directly recruits and serves the students. The EOF Board also oversees a graduate grant program as well as the C. Clyde Ferguson Law and the Martin Luther King Physician-Dentist Scholarships. I was privileged to chair this important educational board for three years, 1997–2000. It continues to be a great pleasure for me to work with EOF's outstanding Executive Director, Dr. Glenn Lang along with Audrey Bennerson, Assistant Director, Jan Flanagan, Program Specialist, dedicated board members and the EOF Professional Association.

In 1995, I was reappointed by Governor Christine Todd Whitman to membership on the EOF Board as well as the New Jersey Student Assistance Board, which administered the tuition aid programs and other state grants-in-aid for New Jersey students. In 1999, the Student Assistance Board and the Office of Student Assistance was absorbed into an authority that administers all the grants, tuition aid, educational investment, and student loans programs called the Higher Education Student Assistance Authority (HESAA). The general mission of HESAA is to provide New Jersey students and families with the financial and informational resources necessary to pursue education beyond high school. Each year HESAA programs assist many thousands of students with grants, scholarships, loans, and information resources. Through HESAA, New Jersey offers one of the most comprehensive student assistance programs in the nation, providing more than $500,000,000 annually in all forms of student aid. I remain on the HESAA Board today and am very much involved in higher education matters in the state.

In 1992, I was invited by members of the Trustee Board to be a member of the Lincoln University Board of Trustees located in Oxford, Pennsylvania. Lincoln is the oldest historically black college/university. It was chartered in Pennsylvania

in 1854 as the Ashmun Institute for the "higher education of colored youth of the male sex of all religious denominations." In 1866 the name of the institution was changed to Lincoln University. Over the years, Lincoln has attracted men, and since 1953, women of all races, creeds, and colors, becoming one of the great institutions of its kind. I served on the board of this outstanding historical institution for two terms of four years each and was extremely active in student affairs, educational development, evaluations, and university governance committees. I thoroughly enjoyed my tenure there and made every effort to make my participation important to the objectives of the university and its students. I was especially proud to serve on that trustee board with some Omega brothers, who were graduates of Lincoln University, like Attorney William King, Walter Chambers, Dr. Ken Sadler, Donn G. Scott, Bill Robinson, Warren R. Colbert, Frank Gihan, and Dr. Ivory V. Nelson, who was president during the second part of my eight-year tenure on the board. In addition, I served on that trustee board with other outstanding Lincoln University graduates, including Sharlene V. Roberson, Adrienne G. Rhone, and Dr. Leonard Bethel.

XXV

Getting Personal Again

There are many things that I have to give my wife Joan credit for. When the well-known poet talks about "let me count the ways," I know they are countless and treasured. Joan has always been sensitive to health problems and medical conditions. In my case, my three brothers all died of complications from heart disease. Joan arranged for me to have regular checkups with Dr. Robert Lauer, a cardiologist at Muhlenberg Regional Medical Center. This was fortuitous because one September morning in 1994, I woke up feeling great. I remember giving Joan a kiss and telling her that I was going to get dressed and go down to the Fanwood A&P and get her a cereal she liked for breakfast. I got down to the store and as soon as I parked the car I began to feel ill. I got out and somehow found a shopping cart nearby and leaned over it while pushing it into the store. I was very uncomfortable and kept thinking that I would just go in and get that one thing and get out as soon as I could do so. I got all the way to the cereals, even looked at the box I wanted, but decided I had better get back to the car and go home. I got in the car, sat down and went into a semi faint with the sensation of having water cascading down over me. As I sat there getting my wits about me and soaking wet down to my waist, I somehow got the car started and carefully drove back to our home on Wood Road. I don't know how I did it. It just must have been God's will. When I turned into the driveway, I saw our dog, Chester, at the front door. I pulled into the garage and began pushing the horn and practically leaning over it in my weakened state.

As often the case, Joan was getting dressed with the radio on. She did not hear the horn. Chester was at the front door and upon seeing the car entering the driveway, raced to the side door that led to the porch and the garage and began barking furiously. Joan finally heard him and went to the garage to see why he was barking. She saw I was inside the car and immediately recognized that I was in trouble. Not wishing to wait for the rescue squad, she called the hospital and told them she was bringing me in and called Dr. Lauer to meet us there. She jumped in the driver's seat and actually shoved me over to the passenger side and drove like mad toward the hospital. She happened to pick a direction that was a short cut, and came upon a policeman talking to a friend. She told him she had to get to the hospital ASAP. He took off with his siren blaring, leading her through crossing traffic, stop signs, and lights all the way to Mulhenberg Regional Medical Center, where the Emergency Room staff was waiting with a stretcher. After evaluating my condition, Dr. Lauer gave me a TPA shot to dissolve the clot. They worked over me for several hours in the Emergency Room. I lost consciousness, almost died, and was not aware of a thing until I opened my eyes hours later in a bed on the Intensive Care floor and saw my beautiful wife looking at me. Many times when I think about that heart attack and about the dog and what Joan did, I break down tearfully and thankfully. I would not be alive today if it were not for a wife who understood my medical situation and a doctor who saved my life. I love her so very much, but I know I can never, never do enough to match even some of her concern and love for me.

I underwent angioplasty while in the hospital in September 1994. However, after a stress test and a heart catheterization in the spring of 1995, it was determined that I needed triple bypass surgery. I was very fortunate to have open-heart surgery performed by a brilliant surgeon, Dr. Haroutune A. Mekhjian, Chief of Cardiac Surgery at St. Joseph's Medical Center in Paterson, New Jersey. Joan was there with me every step of the way, as she has always been, especially in very traumatic situations like this one. When I opened my eyes after being in a recovery room for what seemed like hours, the first vision I saw was Joan looking down at me with that happy life-giving smile of hers.

After months of recuperation, I knew that I would not be able to keep up the large property with the large pool, the big back yard, and the many gumball trees. We opted to move to a townhouse where we didn't have to worry about any outside maintenance. We finally made a decision and moved into a two-story dwelling in a development in North Edison called Timberline.

Joan and I loved the Timberline home until my left hip started to deteriorate in 2000. Walking became increasingly painful and by 2001, I was on a cane and having a hard time going up and down stairs in the townhouse and with walking in general. I knew then that an operation for a replacement in the left hip joint would soon be a necessity. I also began to realize that we could not stay in that two-story townhouse much longer. Joan worked with a realtor and found a single story home in the Rossmoor Adult Community in Monroe, New Jersey. Rossmoor is a well-known, established New England-like development with a golf course, big club house, pools, tennis courts, a coquet field, etc. It is ranked among the 20 best such places in the country.

Today, we are here in Rossmoor. I am still on the two state higher education boards and very active in each. I am still involved with my fraternity on the local, district, and national levels. I was asked to develop a Code of Conduct for the fraternity and did so, presenting the finished product to the presiding Grand Basileus at the Indianapolis Conclave. He gave it to the incoming Grand Counselor, who made a few refinements, reproduced it, and circulated it. I love Omega and will continue to provide advisory support to my chapter, the district, and the fraternity as long as I am able to do so. I will continue periodically to give speeches and presentations at various Omega chapter events speaking to issues that I feel directly impact our fraternity in our efforts to bring continuing brilliance to our four Cardinal Principles, Manhood, Scholarship, Perseverance, and Uplift.

One of the fraternal activities of which I am very proud of is the annual James S. Avery Scholarship Ball that my chapter initiated during the 1990s. My special pride comes from the financial assistance given to young black men and women in

Members of the Omicron Chi Chapter at the chapter's annually sponsored James S. Avery Scholarship Ball, Somerset, NJ, 1998

the Plainfield, New Jersey, area to help them achieve degrees in higher education. Scholarship must always be one of our most important areas of concern, particularly since our world today and tomorrow demands that you have the educational background necessary to succeed in an increasingly technological world. I am so grateful and honored that whatever I have done in life as an Omega man, in fact as a black man, has earned the respect of my beloved fraternity brothers. My hope is that each year, the James S. Avery Scholarship Ball will continue to provide important start up funds for an increasing number of black youth.

Joan is now officially retired. She is now one of the directors of the "Mutual 4C," the name for the group of houses where we live. We are both very much involved in social, political, and religious activities here in the Rossmoor Community. Joan attends one of the Catholic churches in Monroe, and I attend the Rossmoor Community Church, an inter-denominational church, where I am involved in its activities, along with those of three other organizations. Joan is a very talented pianist and plays for a number of organizations at their social events. Joan is also a member of several clubs. When you think about it, we probably have a larger group of friends with whom we associate here than at any place we have lived. Of course, now having our Scottie, "Duncan," does not hurt. He likes people and happily greets everyone he meets, making conversation between the adults very easy.

Since moving to Rossmoor, I am on the way to becoming a Bionic Man. I had a left hip replacement in November 2002 at Robert Wood Johnson University Medical Center in New Brunswick by a very gifted surgeon, Dr. Harwood. In February 2004, I had right shoulder surgery to repair a very serious rotator cuff and bicep muscle injury. This is where my daughter stepped in to oversee my shoulder surgery. Sheryl, who runs Dr. Fredric Kleinbart's office, set me up with this wonderful orthopedic surgeon, who did a spectacular job on an impossible shoulder. After four months of vigorous therapy, I have recovered much of the use of my right arm. Now, if I can just be careful, athletically and otherwise, I think I can stay out of hospitals.

I say often that despite the ups and downs of life, and there have been many, God has certainly blessed me in many, many wonderful ways. I have the greatest wife and an extended family with wonderful children, stepchildren, grandchildren, nieces, and grand nieces and nephews. I have a special bond of friendship and respect with my fraternity brothers, particularly those in my home chapter, that I will always treasure deeply. I am now 82 years old. I don't feel it or, quite frankly, look it. I believe that there is more that I can do to continue to have a positive impact on several aspects of our society. I hope that providence agrees with me.

As a past Grand Basileus of Omega, in fact the 28th Grand Basileus, the second oldest at this time, I feel a strong need to keep focusing the attention of my brothers on critical problem areas in our society. In speech after speech, in varying ways, I point out to them that I firmly believe that organizations like the Omega Psi Phi Fraternity are uniquely positioned in philosophical direction and talent to be the leaders among those working on the serious problems facing our communities and particularly our youth. Organizations like Omega Psi Phi Fraternity, Inc., are going to face some serious challenges in the years ahead, challenges relating to organization, membership makeup, behavior, customs, leadership development, and program relevancy. All such organizations must look at the way its leaders are developed and selected. In essence they must first answer the question, do we continue to determine our international level fraternal leaders on the basis of where they live, or do we come up with a plan to select leaders on the basis of real leadership experience and a set of proven leadership criteria?

Organizations like Omega must make a conscious committed effort to sever relationships with old customs and outdated procedures that now draw the interest of illegality and the courts and sap our fraternal strength. Already, we have seen the impact of legal decisions regarding matters like hazing and actions that are identified, right or wrong, like branding, with it. Legal decisions will be the master of our fate unless we eliminate all behavior and customs that attract legal actions. We simply must sever any future relationship with outdated customs. We must realize that there are no logical reasons for us to continue fascination with actions of any kind that have no real value or intelligent application to the things we should be doing. It is senseless not to come to that realization.

Today's society in so many ways is quite interdependent, affected by problem areas that touch a broad spectrum of humanity. Under such conditions one group cannot do enough alone to really impact major problems. Networking is a logical solution. Groups and organizations must interact with joint efforts to achieve real success on critical urban social problems. In this context, we must simply work diligently at styling our organizational talents and program objectives to effectively impact the needs of particular areas of concern. New, aggressive social alignments are necessary to achieve intensive networking with other socially relevant organizations.

Fortunately, as far as Omega is concerned, there is something that gives continued strength and brilliance to its fraternal character. The four cardinal principles which form the basic foundation of our existence, brought into being almost a century ago, are still central to the kind of conduct and behavior that are linked to successful programming and living. The tenets of scholarship, of manliness, of perseverance, and the religious quality of uplift remain basic to all that we do as an organization and as individuals. The longevity and level of relevancy of Omega's future life, as well as that of other socially oriented organizations, will depend on how we use these principles in reacting to what we seek to accomplish.

The method to guide us to effective change may be a special constitutional convention that would not focus upon a wholesale review from A to Z, but one that would concentrate on particular areas of interest like selection of leadership, membership intake, and fraternal behavior. Within such a context, use of task forces and putting the experience and skills of brothers in proper groupings would make good sense.

If organizations like Omega do not choose to pursue a valid self-assessment, then in doing nothing, two possibilities can occur. On the one hand, we will continue to exist with little real relevance or social significance, or on the other hand, the continuation of stupid, senseless actions will lead to financial ruin and chaos. Neither one of these possibilities should be an option. We have a serious choice to make.

As men of Omega, let us always remember that we did not enter our fraternity to have social tunnel vision. We entered for more relevant reasons that put us right in the middle of the social crises around us. I hope we will rise to our calling as men committed to doing something to raise the level of aspiration of those around us, providing those alert signals and the guidance that can assure safe passage through the onslaught of technological change.

Whatever we do as Omega men, let us do it with a caring spirit reaching out to all people asking them to join hands with men of intelligence and grace to work on issues that can elevate the future promise of human kind.

As many of my fraternity brothers already know, I have never felt that a real, committed Omega man was an ordinary man, but a man set tall in his ways—a man who chose to walk in greatness with other men that he can truly call his brothers. I believe that every calling in life has its normal day-to-day set of things to be done if one is to survive. Beyond that point of day-to-day relations, however, we have that opportunity as Omega men to invest our participation in life with an enduring significance. This is the only way that we as fraternity brothers can attain the dignity and the distinction that leads to the life to which we must all aspire. This is my hope, my wish, and my prayer for the men of the Omega Psi Phi Fraternity, Inc.

There is something else of great significance that I hope the Men of Omega will keep primary in their lives. It is the significance of our fraternal friendship. We say it is "essential to the soul." There is greater meaning in those words, for we must see our friendship as being so strong and binding that it immunizes us from thoughts and actions counter to our cardinal principles, so strong that it prevents misconceptions to creep maliciously into our lives, rule our outlook, and dominate our ambitions.

Consistent with this is our need to rededicate ourselves whenever the situation is appropriate for such a ceremony. When I refer to rededication, it is not just to the vows that we took upon entering our brotherhood, it is our rededication to a grand ideal brought into creation almost 100 years ago. It is our rededication to the way we should live as Omega men. It is our rededication to the culture we seek to emulate and to replicate. It is our rededication to a set of values and standards of a caring, sharing brotherhood. I have endeavored to make my life a living symbol and a model of what is best in Omega.

An autobiography is a very flattering experience since one is essentially writing about himself and not highlighting the things that would be embarrassing. If I have forgotten to include something special that comes to the reader's mind or forgot to mention someone significant in my life, please forgive me. The omission is certainly not intentional.

I want to close with a communication that could serve as some kind of eulogy. It is a letter I received from my lawyer stepson, George Horrigan, on July 27, 2000.

> Dear Jim:
>
> How proud you must be to receive this honor from Cranford. [He is referring to the award from the Cranford Fund for Educational Excellence.] What tremendous accomplishments you have achieved in your life. Think of all the lives you have touched, and as a result, made better.

I hope you realize just how proud your family is of you. Speaking for myself, I could never express just how proud I am of you. To have known such a man as yourself is an honor to me. Today, so many people are confused about who and what a role model should be. Oftentimes people believe someone is a role model because they are an athlete or a musician, but that is far from the truth. In my opinion, a true role model is a person who lives an honorable and ethical life. One who strives to lead others to a better life. You are certainly that person. You have always been, and will always be, one of my role models. I can only hope that as I get older and I look back on my life I can say that I have accomplished half of what you have. Then I will feel that I have had a good life.

As I strive to be a good father to our children, I must look to those people who I admire as a guide. You are one of those people. What a wonderful father you have been. God has given me the opportunity to learn from you, and I try my best to do so.

As time goes by, I will make sure to tell my children and their children about you. I will make it a point to tell them about the things you have accomplished in your life. Not only will I tell them about a man who, despite growing up in a time of extreme discrimination, rose to the top of the American business world, but of the father whom I loved and admired with all of my heart. I love you, Jim.

With all my love,
Your son, George

After the kind things that my stepson George has said, maybe I should just quit while I am ahead. In the time I have left on this earth, though, I think I will keep trying to make a positive difference in the things I do that impact the lives of others.

An Important Addendum

On March 6, 2006, James S. Avery, Sr., received a Jackie Robinson Foundation ROBIE Award for Lifetime Achievements as an African-American trailblazer in Corporate America, for his activities with various national organizations and his accomplishments in the field of higher education. At the same affair, seven other individuals received awards, including the United States senator from the state of New York, Senator Hillary Rodham Clinton, who received her ROBIE Award for Humanitarianism. The awards were presented at the organization's 2006 Annual Awards Dinner, which was held in the grand ballroom of the Waldorf Astoria Hotel, New York City, New York. Bill Cosby, entertainer and philanthropist, was the master of ceremonies. Danny Glover, actor and activist, introduced Jim and the other corporate trailblazers.

The Jackie Robinson Foundation, created in 1973 by Rachel Robinson, wife of the Major League Baseball Hall of Famer, is a public, not-for-profit organization that assists increasing numbers of minority youths through the granting of scholarships for higher education and career and leadership development programs.

The coveted Lifetime Achievement Award is the Foundation's highest tribute to a person who has devoted their life to improving the circumstances of others through equal opportunity, fighting for social justice, and giving back to the community.

Other Photographs of Interest in the Life of James S. Avery

Happy Birthday to You!

Brother Grand, receiving sculpted faces of the Founders of Omega Psi Phi Fraternity, Inc.

Second district council members and past district representatives were plentiful at this night of celebration

Brother Grand, expressing thanks at 82nd Birthday Celebration

Brother Grand with his Chapter Basileus, Brother Morris Lucky from Omicron Chi

Omicron Chi Chapter Brothers presenting gifts to Brother Grand

Brothers of Omega, proud to be a part of Brother Grand's Celebration

People We've Come to Know

Some Omega leaders with former NAACP president and civil rights activist Brother Reverend Benjamin Hooks

Jim Avery and (R–L) former Manhattan Burrough president Percy Sutton, Brother Richard Green, and past Grand Basileus Brother George Meares

Brother Jim Avery flanked by (R) Brother Earl Graves, publisher of Black Enterprise Magazine, and (L) Earl's son, Brother John Graves

Brother Avery with (L–R) Brother Roy Wilkins, former National Executive Director of the NAACP, Brother Lloyd Bell, and Brother Harold Cooke, former National Executive Secretary of Omega Psi Phi Fraternity

Brother Grand and Brother Milt Johnson pose with well-known comedian and Omega Brother Bill Cosby

Brother Avery and Senator Edward Brooke of Massachusetts, the first African-American to be popularly elected to the U.S. Senate

Brother Grand and the ever-present civil rights advocate and CEO of Operation PUSH, Brother Jesse L. Jackson

Omega Psi Phi Grand Basilei (Past and Present)

Grand Basileus George H. Grace and Brother Avery at the St. Louis, MO conclave

Brother Rudy Powell (L) and Brother Alexander Barnes (R) stand with Past Grand Basilei Corbett, Avery, and Meares

Brother Eddie Taylor (c) stands with Grand Basileus Grace and Past Grand Basilei Braynon, Livingston, Avery, Gilmore, and Norman

Past Grand Basilei Moses C. Norman, Herbert Tucker, Edward Braynon, Jim Avery, Burnel Coulon, and Benjamin Livingston

Grand Basilei Coulon, Livingston, Braynon, Avery, and Norman pose with former National Executive Secretary Brother H. Carl Moultrie (3rd from left)

1974—Omicron Chi Basileus Lavell Sutherland presents Appreciation Award to Brother Avery for his service to the fraternity as grand basileus while Past Grand George E. Meares, Past DR Milt Johnson, and NES Brother H. Carl Moultrie look on

Brother Avery passes the gavel to incoming Grand Basileus Judge Marion Garnett

2004—Kappa Omicron Fraternity House in New York City with second district officers (from left): Brother James D. Edmonds, III, DKRS; Brother Marvin Dillard, 1st Vice District Representative; Brother Grand; Brother Gregory Ackles, District Representative, and Brother Marvin Cobles, Asst. KF

Former second district representatives with notable brothers Rudy Powell and Eddie Taylor

(L to R) Jim and Joan Avery and Brother Bob Early, former second district counselor

Members of Alpha Nu Chapter, Stamford, Connecticut area, circa 1981

(L to R) Grand Keeper of Records and Seal Brother Terrel Parris presents a Supreme Council Award to Brother Jim Avery at the Iota Xi Chapter's "Elders Honoree Awards Banquet" as past award recipients Eddie Taylor, Rudy Powell, and Nate Thomas look on

The beloved Brother Rudy Powell and his lovely wife, Lucy, pose with Brother Grand

Brothers of Omicron Chi Chapter, Plainfield, New Jersey area, circa 1990

(L to R) Former DR Brother Andrew Ray, Past Grand Basileus Moses C. Norman, Past Grand Basileus Jim Avery, Former NES John Epps and Past Grand Basileus C. Tyrone Gilmore surround Brother William H. Cosby (3rd from left) at his fraternal initiation into Beta Alpha Alpha Chapter, Westchester, New York

Members of Iota Xi Chapter surround Elder Honor Awardees Nate Thomas, Eddie Taylor, and Jim Avery

Brother Morris Lucky, Basileus, Omicron Chi, Brother Judge James A. Key, Brother Grand, and Brother Mark Meyers

(L to R) Howard Woods, Editor of the St. Louis August, *Hobart Taylor, Jr., Asst. to President Lyndon B. Johnson, Jim, and Don Thomas of Chrysler Corporation at Plans for Progress Meeting, 1965*

The ESSO Public Relations Team, 1956 (Jim Avery and Wendell P. Alston)

EXXON Operations Department Representative reviewing product distribution in the Northeastern Region with public affairs manager James S. Avery, Sr.

Jim Avery (3rd from left) with other EXXON managers before going down into a coal mine in Western Illinois

Brother Grand with a portrait of his father

Jim Avery (3rd from left), Chairman of NY State Petroleum Council, looks on as Barbara Wallace, on the Council's staff, presents Speakers Award to Bob Brown of Exxon Corporation

Family Pictures

Jim and Joan, still in love after all these years

Jim Avery's granddaughter Kelly as cheerleader of South Brunswick High

Jim Avery's niece, Sandra Avery

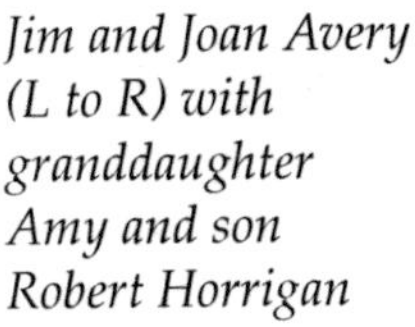

Jim and Joan Avery (L to R) with granddaughter Amy and son Robert Horrigan

Brother Grand with daughter Sheryl Avery

Former teacher Jim Avery (center) with members of the Cranford High School Class of 1953 at their 50th Reunion Gala

Former teacher Jim Avery (rear) with a group of former students of Cranford High School

Richard "Duke" Armstrong and John "Jack" Phanne, two of coach Jim Avery's former football players at Cranford High

Joan and Jim Avery at a Cranford High School gathering of former students

Jim Avery with Vinnie Vicci and Jesse Bell, two of Jim's former football players at Cranford High School

(L to R) Mrs. Joan Avery, Brother Felmon Motley, former Second District Director of Public Relations, and Brother Grand

Former teacher Jim Avery, front and center again, with members of the Cranford High School Class of 1954 at their 50th Reunion Celebration

Three of Coach Jim Avery's roughneck football players of Cranford High School, (L to R) George Rogers, Vinnie Vicci, and Bob Bolomey

Jim Avery's lifelong buddy Thomas L. (Steve) Stevenson

Joan and Jim Avery seated at right with members of his Cranford High School Class of 1941 at its 50th reunion. To the rear and left is Jim's high school basketball coach, Ben Carnevale

Bishop Edgar Amos Love

One of Jim Avery's most beloved and respected friends and brothers. Brother Love was one of the four founders of the Omega Psi Phi Fraternity, Incorporated, which was founded on November 17, 1911. Jim was privileged to be the fraternity's 28th grand basileus (national president) from 1970 to 1973

Printed in the United States
65871LVS00008BA/90

9 781587 365782